The Way He Loves Me

Dawna P Renne

Edited by
Nancy Plum Tuthill
Amy Grace Renne

Tracy,
May you always
be amazed at the
way He loves you!

Love,
Dawna
3/24/15

Permissions:

Cover photo credit: Matt Novak,
Back cover photo credit: Amy Renne,
Cover design: Chris Renne

Acknowledgments

Without the help of four very gifted people this book and its revision would never have been completed. I thank my mother, Nancy Plum Tuthill, for her diligence and dedication in editing. Your skill in this task is invaluable. I thank my children, also: Chris Renne, for my birthday gifts of the foreword and cover artwork; Amy Grace Renne, for her creative design and layout of the text, and for the description of my book found on the back cover.

I thank Ralph Venezia for his scrutiny of and suggestions for modification of the first printing which has led to this revised version.

Also, thank you all for your encouragement, reassurance and inspiritment. The Lord has used you mightily in this project.

THE WAY HE LOVES ME

Table of Contents

THE WAY HE LOVES ME

Introduction

This book was written over a period of two years, which were two of the most difficult years of my life. Now that I'm on the other side of it, the book is finished and my trials have eased up, I feel blessed. I hope the readers of my story will see how amazing and wonderful our God is--especially in the ways He shows up in our lives. I thank Him and bless His Name for allowing me to be a part of His plan.

The stories in this book are personal and real. I share the good, the bad and the ugly in my life and especially in my marriage in hopes that someone reading it will be able to relate and to be encouraged. Women especially will find similarities to their experiences. Men may be able to gain insight into their wives' ways of thinking.

As many of these stories include my husband, Mark, I want to set the record straight at the beginning that even though I share my frustrations with him throughout our marriage God has done an amazing work in us and at this point, after almost thirty years of living together, I am madly, head-over-heals in love with Mark. He is an amazingly talented, caring, faithful husband. I've learned over the years that there is no one in my mind or heart that compares with him. I can't thank the Lord enough for keeping us together and teaching us how to love each other as He has shown us the way He loves us.

THE WAY HE LOVES ME

Foreword

By Chris Renne

When the term "Woman of Faith" comes up one thinks of the obvious Bible heroes... Esther, Ruth, Mary. This is the story of a new hero. A woman so relatable, so transparent, so real, that you can't help but add her to that list in the future. The difference is that in the Bible stories the woman in question is portrayed as practically perfect. You don't hear about them losing their temper, struggling with real life pressures, or having to change diapers. This story, however, hits so close to home that you can't ignore it's testimony. This is the spiritual autobiography of the woman I not only call my mother, but also my dear friend.

She always told me, as a child, to "look it up" if I didn't know something. I'd grumble my way to the bookshelf and search the encyclopedia set or dictionary for whatever I needed to know. I complained at the time, because I just wanted her to tell me, but I now see that knowledge is better retained when searched out instead of merely heard. Fast forward to now--I'm still "looking it up" every time I don't understand something, but the medium is different. Smartphones have revolutionized the way we absorb information; my google search history is equal parts hilarious and ridiculous, but my thirst for knowledge is one of the things I am so grateful that my mother instilled in me as a child.

This book has the potential to be a reference text of sorts... A handbook for this generation. It champions the everyday woman. From the 18 year old girl without a clue to the seasoned Christian mother, and everyone in between. Although written from a female's perspective, men of all ages will also appreciate the incredible story she has to tell.

As a music producer, people often send me their music for critique or advice or opinion. More often than not, I have to find a way to delicately and respectfully tell them that they may want to pursue a different hobby. When my dear mother came to me with her book for review, I was somewhat concerned. This is my mother's first attempt at writing a book and I did not know what to expect. I wasn't surprised when I picked it up and immediately realized that she had hit a home run. Top of the Billboard charts hit single. You'll see what I mean.

The most powerful concept in this text is how God continually uses my mother over and over again--flaws and all. In our weakness, He is strong.

If you ever meet Dawna, you will love her. Her charisma and joy are contagious. The love this woman has for her Savior and her family is inspiring. If you already know her, give her a call and let her know that you're about to read her book.

This book is going to encourage you. It's going to motivate you. It's going to get you through some tough times. It's going to help bring peace in the worst of times. It's going to help you realize that He is in control, and He loves you more than you will ever know, even if you don't love Him back.

Now, it gives me great pleasure to introduce to you, the amazing story of an incredible woman of God, and how her true Father's love has been put on brazen display throughout her life. Get comfortable, because you won't be able to put it down.

THE WAY HE LOVES ME

Prologue

Thirty years!   That's the longest I've ever persevered at one thing.   My brother once said to me, "You quit everything you've ever started." He was right, for the most part. I often wondered what would become of me since it seemed I couldn't stay committed to anything.

However, we were both wrong in at least one area. I have stayed committed in my faith and trust in Jesus, the Christ, the only begotten Son of God. It has been thirty years! My relationship with Him has had its tests over those years, and I've made mistakes along the way, but I've never ceased to believe that Jesus was born of a virgin, died on the cross for the salvation of myself and "whosoever believes", rose again from the dead, is now seated at the right hand of the Father and is interceding for me. What that means in actuality and in all of its perfection of God's ways I don't know, but I trust God to have it all worked out so that I don't have to know exact details.

Thirty years! I'm still amazed when I think about it. I would add that they have been thirty years of love that I never imagined I could experience.   His love for me is relentless and unfathomable! I'll never totally understand it. What I do know and what has been graciously revealed to me is what this book is about.   God has asked, permitted and commanded me to share stories about our relationship that have proved to me time and time again the way He loves me.

A few months ago I was sitting in my favorite chair in my room where I spend my early time reading my Bible. As I was praying, talking and listening to my Father I felt the need to write down my story, especially the trials I had just been through. I began typing on my iPad starting with a title and shooting out about five paragraphs.   I suddenly stopped, thinking, "What a waste of time! I have so much to do and who would read this anyway? " I closed my iPad and forgot about it.

A month later as my husband, Mark and I endured a discouragement that would not subside I cried out to God to give us, especially my husband, encouragement. It was a Saturday night and I prayed that Mark would be intimately blessed by Him so that he would be able to get through this difficult time. I have learned that a touch from the Lord is worth more than anything this world has to offer in bringing comfort to a hurting soul.

The next day at church our Father met us and did exceedingly and abundantly above all I could have ever thought or imagined. The music and sermon were extraordinarily pertinent to our situation. At the end of the sermon the pastor gave an invitation to those who felt they needed a special touch from God to come up to the altar. I stood praying that Mark would go forward where I thought God could bless him, as had happened so many times before, but this time I felt that it was urgent. Mark didn't budge. As I kept praying I suddenly felt a peace come over me that I have come to recognize as God's presence overwhelming me. At that point I thought, "Maybe I'm supposed to go up and Mark will follow me." So I went towards the pastor joining about fifty others.

After the pastor prayed over all of us he began to give personal ministry to individuals which means he had a message from God for specific people. He asked if anyone had just recently been diagnosed with cancer and a woman in the front of the crowd raised her hand. I closed my eyes and raised my hands joining the pastor and others in prayer for this woman. When he finished praying for her, with my eyes still closed, I heard him call out another woman. At the same time I felt someone, an usher, touch my elbow. As I opened my eyes the pastor was looking and pointing at me.

I was stunned as he called me up to the platform so he could pray over me. After the first sentence I fell to my knees because I knew without a doubt that God was speaking through this man as he said:

> *"You feel so out of sorts, you feel like 'God, I have so much inside of me for You and Your work.' In fact I'm looking at a vision and in the vision I see you are writing and you stopped, you interrupted your writing, you're writing a book-- just a motivational book, a book that encourages people, you feel like 'I have lots of little stories and lots of little neat sayings that can encourage people', and you stopped writing because you felt like 'Who wants to read my book?' The Lord says 'Finish what I've put in your heart to do, my Daughter. Because indeed I will allow you to fulfill that which is a burden of your heart. And you will be known as the consummate encourager. You are an encourager! I give you a ministry to women, it will encourage women, it will help them come out of hardship and in the latter days it will branch over into men and children, but it will start off with ministry to women. It will encourage the heart and help them go through life with strength and hope.' Receive today the anointing of the Holy Spirit."*

My heart was so full of joy and peace and assurance that God was so intimately involved in my life that I had no reason to be discouraged. As my family and I discussed this, my husband was encouraged, which was the answer to my prayer. Again, I was amazed by the way He loves me.

I pray that as you read this book you, too, will realize that God's love which was manifested through His Son, Jesus Christ, is limitless; and He is relentless and specific in the way He loves you.

THE WAY HE LOVES ME

Chapter One

BEGINNINGS

"This is what the past is for! Every experience God gives us, every person He puts in our lives is the perfect preparation for the future that only He can see."

-Corrie Ten Boom

"It's not religion! It's relationship!" That's one of

my favorite Christian clichés. But just what does a relationship with God look like anyway? Can a human being actually relate personally to the One Who contrived the universe and all it contains? Does the Consummator of all time and being really want to be involved in the everyday affairs of a woman like me?

Where does one begin to tell a story that, according to scripture, began in God's mind before one of my days came to be?

Perhaps I should start at the very beginning with my childhood and all the "stuff" that entailed...the good, the bad and the ugly. Every family has "stuff". I have learned that my Father in Heaven has sovereignly placed me in my family in His timing and in the place of His choosing. All of it according to Romans 8:28 was to work together for my good. I may touch on some of these stories later but for now I would like to start somewhere else. Somewhere that was a pivotal turning point in my life, though I did not realize it at the time.

It was 1984 and I was twenty-three years old. Three and a half years earlier, at the age of nineteen, I had married. Only a few months into the marriage, due to our vast immaturity, it started to crumble and was completely annihilated by 1984. I was an emotional train-wreck. In 1982 I had come to a believing faith in Jesus Christ and for a while it seemed like my life was coming together. However, it actually got worse. I read a book a few years later that explained this phenomenon. It expressed the idea that when we live in the world, in the flesh, in sin, before salvation, it's like when Rambo trudged through the swamp and emerged covered with mud and slime. When we believe in Jesus and His death on the cross for salvation it's like emerging from the swamp and all the muck and mire is hosed off. However, there are leeches that have become attached to us that need to be picked off one by one. The amount of leeches affixed to us is dependent upon how long we waded through the muck (sinful lifestyle). I had quite a few leeches that needed to be detached. By 1984 I had thrown my faith out the window, so to speak; "It didn't work for me". What I really meant was God wasn't doing what I wanted Him to do.

My marriage was annihilated but not terminated. I had never bothered to get divorced. I was in and out of one relationship after another, many of them just "one night stands". I lived one cliché after the other: "If it feels good, do it", "Looking for love in all the wrong places"; "If you can't be with the one you love, love the one you're with." "You only live once." Then finally: "You reap what you sow"...

It was Halloween and I was employed as a commuter bus driver to New York City. After depositing my passengers at the gate I took a break and perused the merchandise through the windows of the not yet open shops of Port Authority. As I headed toward the stairs that led back to my bus, I noticed another driver, from a different bus company. The company was known in bus driver circles of the time as top notch and one only "got in" if they "knew someone". I decided I was going to "know someone" in the company so I struck up a conversation with the driver. His name was Mark. By the time we reached his bus, which was parked a few gates down from mine, I felt like I had known him forever. I gave him my phone number and drove home on Cloud Nine.

This is the part of the story that I'm a little embarrassed to tell as I think about how little regard I had for my life, though now I look back and laugh. Mark and I had planned our first date for that Saturday night. We were going camping. When Saturday came around I realized that I didn't know this guy from Joe Schmoe and for all I knew he could be a serial killer. So I got a bright idea! I left a note in my apartment that read, "To whom it may concern, I am going camping with Mark Renne and if anything happens to me--he did it!" and I left his phone number.

As it turned out, our date was wonderful and I didn't get murdered. We got to know each other, had lots of fun and all the way home we talked and laughed and I felt so happy. Our relationship advanced rapidly and a few weeks later, on the eve before Thanksgiving, we were talking about marriage. There wasn't any proposal or anything extremely romantic happening. We were talking about marriage because I had found a list on his dining room table. It said things like "surfing, diving, camping, fishing, motorcycle rides, marriage, kids." I asked him, "What is this?" He said it was a list of things he was thinking he'd like to do with me. When I drew attention to the "marriage and kids" part he admitted his desire to pursue those with me. I told him flat out I couldn't marry him because he wasn't a Christian. I stated matter-of-factly, "I know that I am not doing what I should be but I believe some day I will be back on track with the Lord and I won't marry anyone who is not a Christian." (Being twenty-three I thought I had my life all figured out.) He asked me what that meant. I was so new at this "Christian" stuff, I wasn't exactly sure what it meant. I tried to explain it to him by sharing the story of what happened to me.

Two years earlier, I had come to a place of utter despair, turmoil permeating my life. I was separated from my husband at the time, living at home, which was somewhat functionally-challenged. One day, I was working for my parents in their picture framing store. I was organizing the mat board storage rack and contemplating my miserable life. I heard someone call my name. I even turned around to see who it was but no one was there.

"Why don't you go talk with someone from Barbara's church?"

Barbara was my mother-in-law and I had been intrigued by her peaceful demeanor when there was much upheaval in her life because of the choices her family members had made. However, I argued with the voice:

Why would I do that? They are all nuts!

I didn't hear the voice again. I wondered what had just happened. I had never really heard God's voice before. I had only had thoughts that I thought maybe were God communicating with me but I couldn't be sure. This time was one of the first lessons in that area. I have learned over the years that a tell-tale sign of the Lord speaking to me is, I tend to argue first, listen later.

After contemplating the fact that God was trying to communicate with me I started thinking about this idea of going to see someone from Barb's church. Maybe if I went to see them I would get in the good graces of my in-laws, I could get back together with my husband and my life would be good. So I asked Barbara if she knew anyone with whom

I could speak.   She gave me the phone number of an older couple, Mr. and Mrs. John Reed.   By the time I entered their living room, on August 24, 1982,   I had already conspired and decided I was going to do whatever it took to get back with my husband.   That sounds noble, but it really wasn't because I wasn't thinking of him, I was thinking of myself and wanted to get out of my difficult situation at home. I now see how similar I was to Jacob in the Bible, conniving and deceiving to get my way.

The gentleman asked me why I had come to see him and what came forth from my mouth was a barrage of complaints against everyone in my life that had ever hurt me. I hadn't planned on that. I don't know what brought it on, but I let it all out. He listened patiently.

When I had finished, I was crying profusely. His kind wife handed me some tissues, but that was all the sympathy I received. I am glad for that. They didn't allow me to wallow in self pity. That would not have helped me at all. Mr. Reed proceeded to explain to me that the Bible said

> "...all have sinned and fallen short of
> the glory of God." (Romans 3:23)

I calculated that "all" included me.   As he continued he explained that just as all those people had hurt me I had hurt God with my own actions.   Then he showed me that the "wages of sin is death". (Romans 6:23) Because of my own sin, I deserved death.   However, because God loved me so much and didn't want me to end up separated from Him forever, which is what would happen if I got what I deserved, He allowed His one and only Son to go to death in my place. He told me if I believed this I would become a child of God (John 1:12) and all my sins would be forgiven and I could live with God forever. Then he asked if I would like to pray and ask Jesus to become my Savior and Lord. I said, "Yes."

Up to this point, I was right back on track with my plan. I knew before I went to the Reeds' house that I was going to become "born-again" like my in-laws, whatever that meant. I had contrived it, which was my usual M.O., trying to get my own way! What I hadn't taken into account was coming into the Presence of the Almighty God, The Creator and Sustainer of the Universe. All of a sudden I realized I was really talking to a personal God, One Who knew my every thought. I couldn't lie to Him. I couldn't connive anything in His Presence. As Mr. Reed led me in what is typically called the Sinner's Prayer, I repeated the words on the outside but on the inside I said, "Lord, You know I've been taught something different all my life but if this is Your Truth, I want to believe it."

At that moment something happened that I really can't explain. A feeling came over me. It was light, and refreshing, and something I had never felt before. I wondered what it was and if it would last. When I woke up the next morning I was thrilled that the "feeling" hadn't gone away. I truly was a different person. I wasn't sure what it all meant but I knew something amazing happened to me that August afternoon.

After I shared my experience with Mark he said he had been thinking about God a lot lately and he wanted what I had. I remember thinking, "Yeah, right. You just want to impress me." Thankfully, I didn't express my true thoughts and led him in a prayer, simply introducing him to faith in Jesus. He later told me that as we held hands, kneeling in front of his couch, he felt something like electricity running between us. To this day he counts that as his conversion experience.

The Way He Teaches Me 1

1. Life before Christ is like Rambo in the swamp: After Christ all the muck is washed away (sin forgiven) but leeches (fleshly/sinful habits) need to be removed one by one.

2. A tell tale sign I'm hearing from the Lord: I argue first, listen later.

Chapter Two

TRAPPED

"When someone intensely desires to obey God's direction,
somehow God manages to get through to that person"
-Catherine Marshall

In December I decided to move in with Mark. My dear friend and roommate, Lynn, who loved the Lord and loved me, tried to convince me that what I was doing was against God's will and His Word. She lovingly showed me scriptures and pleaded with me to reconsider. Years later she told me she had prayed for days about talking to me and was so afraid I'd be angry with her. Being so steeped in my selfish desires I didn't even understand what she was saying. She said she was so surprised how nice I was. Now I realize I wasn't nice, I was blind! Not only because "Love is blind" but sin also makes us blind to what God is trying to tell us.

After moving in with Mark life didn't get easier. I got depressed. On Christmas Day I cried because I realized I was so far from where I wanted to be. I didn't know exactly what that was but I felt like I had missed something. The Holy Spirit was tugging at my heart but I didn't realize it yet.

In January I started getting sick. I was still driving the bus and the fumes made me so nauseous I was afraid I wouldn't be able to keep my breakfast down. I had a hard time staying awake, also. When I finally went to the doctor and he revealed I was pregnant, I was exceedingly shocked. All the years I was married and all the other men I had been with, I had never used birth control. I just assumed I could never have children.

When I walked out of the doctor's office, Mark asked me what he said. I said, "How's 'Daddy' sound?"

Mark is a rather "balanced" sort of guy. He never gets really angry or really happy. It's one of the traits I've grown to love about him. That day he had what I've learned to be a typical Mark reaction. He said, "Cool." and drove me home.

I, on the other hand, was a basket case. First, I was ecstatic. Then the reality hit me. What a huge mess! I was still married to another man. I wasn't even sure Mark was the "one" for me. We didn't have a lot of money. What about my job?

For a split second I thought about abortion. Ironically it was January, the month when Roe vs. Wade had been settled and the Supreme Court deemed abortion a fundamental right under the United States Constitution. And doubly ironic--just the year before I had attended the March for Life which protested that decision. Now I was face to face with the decision of what to do with an unplanned pregnancy. Would my talk become my walk? I understood firsthand what this debate was about. Thankfully, I decided quickly that I would carry this baby to term. Then what?!

God was starting to get my attention again. I decided I better start listening.

Mark wanted to marry me. I had to get divorced first, of course. I called my husband and asked him if he wouldn't mind divorcing me. He was very amiable and somehow I didn't even have to show up at the proceedings.

The simple wedding took place in March. We were married in Mark's parents' home that his mother and sister decorated so beautifully. As friends and family gathered around I quoted the scriptures from Ruth, that I had memorized:

> Intreat me not to leave thee, or to return from following after thee: for whither thou goest, I will go; and where thou lodgest, I will lodge: thy people shall be my people, and thy God my God: Where thou diest, will I die, and there will I be buried: the Lord do so to me, and more also, if ought but death part thee and me. Ruth 1:16-17

Our marriage got off to a rocky start from the get-go. I was so nauseous and cranky on our honeymoon I think Mark wished he had brought someone else! I learned that my new husband had much to learn about being compassionate. He learned that his wife had much to learn about being pleasant! When we got home things weren't much better. We just seemed to bring out the worst in each other.

Mark went to the Lamaze classes with me but made sure I knew how much he disliked them with every breath he took. Then I was wishing I had brought someone else. It didn't help matters at all when one night on the way home from Lamaze, a former girlfriend flagged Mark down and he pulled over to say hello. Here I was, fat, and feeling really ugly while he's chatting with an old flame. The worst night was when he didn't show up at all. He was supposed to meet me at the class but as time ticked on there I was with no partner. He walked in towards the end of the class. I was burning with anger! He calmly stated he had a great excuse. Our boat had burnt up! We had purchased an old fiberglass boat with an outboard motor and friends of Mark's had let him dock it at their house on the lake. Apparently, it was a case of spontaneous combustion, the fire bursting out in the front of the boat and melting the vessel down to the water line.

The only thing left was the outboard motor. However, when he told me, I really thought he was making it up just so he didn't have to come to class. I eventually came to terms with the truth.

I think there were times, many times, when we felt trapped. Neither of us had expected nor anticipated to be married so soon with a baby on the way. Our families were all in turmoil over the situation. We had internal and external pressures causing great angst and confusion. Nobody seemed happy.

A few months after we learned we were pregnant we rented a small house in the same town in which we lived. It was one of three identical houses situated across the street from a farm. I believe they had been built as homes for the farm workers, back in the day. They were just square houses with four rooms— two bedrooms, kitchen, living room and a bathroom in the middle. To us it was paradise because we had a huge yard.

As it turned out the best part was our neighbors, Jim and Harlene Brown. They were Southern Baptists and invited us to church. Since my conversion I had been Brethren, Pentecostal and Presbyterian. Mark and I accepted their invitation and we became part of the Baptist family. The women took to me like mother-hens, teaching me how to be a mother, and most importantly teaching me about Jesus and the Bible. Some of the leeches started coming off.

One day a couple of the women stopped by with some refreshments. As we were chatting the subject came up of how long I'd been married. I was embarrassed to tell them I was married only three months and yet I was six months pregnant, so I lied. I told them I was married for over a year.

After they left I started feeling very guilty. This was a new sensation for me. I had lied most of my life prior to inviting Christ into my life. I didn't like the feeling of guilt. It got worse and worse. Finally, I couldn't take it any longer. I

THE WAY HE LOVES ME

confessed to each woman that I had lied and the truth was I had gotten pregnant before I got married. Those precious women loved me just the same and I learned some valuable lessons. One of which was, now that I had come back to my faith in Jesus, He kept me on a short leash. He wasn't about to let me get away with anything that would hinder my relationship with Him. The Bible says in Psalm 66:18:

> "If I regard iniquity in my heart, the Lord will not hear me."

He wanted me to overcome the sin that I held on to so that He could be my source of all joy.

When I went into labor on September 6th, my due date, I called Harlene. She had said she would drive me when the time came. Mark was still on his bus run so I telephoned his dispatcher to ask him to tell Mark to meet me at the hospital. He was instantly concerned and asked why.

"Oh, it's ok, I'm just having a baby." I replied.

"What?! Are you ok? Do you want me to send a driver over?"

I pictured this big bus pulling up in front of our tiny house.

"No, that won't be necessary. I have a ride, thank you. Just let Mark know."

The scene at our house that evening was quite comical. My labor pains were five minutes apart and not too strong but the doctor just wanted to be safe so he told me to come in. Later I found he had five other women in labor and I think he just wanted to get us all done at once! So even though I wasn't in intense labor, Harlene and Jim made sure they were not going to deliver this baby. They ran around like chickens trying to get everything in the car. Jim carefully got me in the passenger seat. I laughed so hard though when he ran around to the other side to help his wife get in and closed the door on her leg in his haste.   It was just like something from a Steve Martin movie.

Our ride to the hospital was joyous and exciting. I was so thrilled when Harlene prayed for us--Mark, the baby and me--while she drove. She dropped me off at the hospital and Mark was already there. Everything fell so nicely into place.

One of the women in our church was pregnant the same time as I. She was due in late August, I in early September. She and her husband were such a sweet Christian couple. I enjoyed spending time with them.   The husband would spend time with Mark and found things they had in common. The woman's first name was Margaret but I can't remember her husband's name. However, I thank God for them both as they gave us a role model. As it turned out after we had arrived at the hospital and were settled into our room, and while I was having a labor pain, I glanced out the hospital room door and saw Margaret's husband walking down the hallway. Margaret was in labor as well! Both babies were born within a few hours of each other on September 7th, which happened to be the woman's birthday as well. With a few requests to the nurses we were allowed to room together. I never could have planned this better if I tried.

Our baby boy, Christopher James, was beautiful, though isn't every baby so to its mother? He looked like Mark at first then he looked more like me but now everyone says he looks like a dark haired Mark. Giving birth to him was one of the most amazing moments of my life.

Being roommates with Margaret allowed the people from church to visit us simultaneously. Other than them, and our parents for a brief visit, I had no visitors. Margaret had her mom coming to stay with her for a few days when she went home. She was anxious to get home. I on the other hand, had no one to help me as my parents still had five children aged thirteen to nineteen at home and a business to run. I was hoping I could stay at the hospital for a while. I was actually scared to go home with this fragile little bundle of joy. I was afraid I wouldn't know what to do. I had changed my brothers' and sister's diapers hundreds of times, but now that it was my own child, and I was totally responsible for his welfare, I was a nervous wreck. I had to ask the nurse to give me instructions on the basics of baby care. I was clueless! As we drove home from the hospital the tears just started to flow.

The Way He Teaches Me 2

1. God keeps me on a short leash.

2. If I regard sin in my heart, God won't hear my prayers.

3. God's plans are so much better than my own.

Chapter Three

TEARS

"Sometimes the bad things that happen in our lives put us directly on the path to the best things that will ever happen to us."

-Unknown

When I moved in with Mark it didn't completely register that I would be living over an hour away from my friends and family. Mark was, and still is, handsome, fun-loving and very entertaining. The absence of anyone else was never really noticeable. Mark's parents were quite distressed at the prospect of their first grandchild living in a four room "shack" so they purchased a lovely bi-level which we would rent from them. It was wonderful to have more room and for Mark to have a garage where he could store his toys and work on the cars. However, this house was even further away from my loved ones. Later I learned that this was my first of several "desert experiences".

A desert experience is a time when all of the things and people that are familiar and comfortable are taken away and it's just you and God. It seems dry and lonely when we are going through one. Moses spent forty years in his first. God was getting him ready for the biggest adventure of his life. I feel I can relate with Moses in some respects. Moses knew God had great plans for his life. He thought he had it all figured out. He took matters into his own hands. Then when things didn't go exactly as he had planned he ran away. I wonder if he planned to be away only a short period of time or, on the other hand, if he thought he was gone for good, never going back. The Bible doesn't explain what happened during those 40 years but what sticks out to me is, IT WAS FORTY YEARS!!! I'm very thankful my first time in the desert was much shorter.

As I endured this time of isolation, and I discerned that I was going through a desert experience like Moses, I resigned myself to whatever God had for me. I decided that I would not throw a pity party and I would make the best of it. That was the plan at first anyway. I didn't realize there was so much NOT in my favor that remaining firm in that decision would be more difficult than I thought I could bear.

One thing I didn't take into account was hormones! Years later I learned about them but at the time I had no idea that my sadness, especially right after the birth of our son, was attributed to them. Mark and I laugh now about the time he was fixing the ceiling fan and he asked me to hand him a screwdriver. Chris was a few weeks old. As I reached to get the tool I started crying. Mark looked down from the ladder and asked me why I was crying and I just sobbed and said, "I (sniff) don't (sniff) know!" At the time it was heart wrenching to me. We knew nothing about postpartum depression. Apparently I had a good dose of it.

Another thing I didn't consider was my husband's worldview. He was a young man, whose goal in life was just to enjoy as much as he could. He told me he drove a bus because it paid the most for doing the least. He loved to drive, it was easy, and didn't take too much thought. He never went to college but instead joined the army right out of high school. He was stationed in two delightful locations-- Colorado, where he skied, and Hawaii, where he surfed. He was an M.P. serving during peacetime. When Mark became a Christ-follower and started going to church some things started to rock his boat--things he didn't like. For instance, he learned that as a believer in Christ, one of the first things the church expected him to do was get baptized.

According to the pastor of the church we attended at the time, baptism is not a requirement for salvation however it is often described as an act of obedience as Jesus himself told his followers to make disciples, baptizing them in the name of the Father, the Son and the Holy Spirt. I have viewed it in this way: the first man was given only one command to obey. He could do anything else he wanted to do except for the one thing God told him not to do. Jesus said, "If you love Me, you will keep My commandments." So we can surmise that God equates obedience with love. We show God that we love Him by our surrendering to His will and desires. Many a woman has surrendered everything to a man just to show she loves him, often in a wrong way. How easy it would have been for Man and Woman to do just one thing to show they loved God. Just one little thing: Don't eat of "the tree of the knowledge of good and evil"! But, after listening to the lies of the Adversary (Satan), just like a defiant child who can't stand to be told "don't", they did it, proving that they didn't love God as much as they said they did. I wonder if they ever stopped to consider that the consequences would separate them from God forever. Disobedience is called sin. Sin and God can't stand in the same place. Therefore, sinners and God can't be together.

God proved He loved Man more. He knew Man would fail to submit so from the beginning He had the plan set forth that He would send His Son, Jesus, to pay the ransom to give Mankind the chance to come back to Himself. All who believe and trust Jesus have the privilege to go back to God, the Father. The Bible says:

> "God gave us eternal life, and this life is in His Son. He who has the Son has the life; he who does not have the Son of God does not have the life." 1 John 5:11,12 (NET)

Once Man gets back to God, now what? Do we just live like nothing ever happened? After a wife has cheated on her husband can he just say "I forgive you and I trust you."? Not likely. He may forgive but it will take time and proof for him to trust. In a similar way, God has a way of getting us back on track to show once again we love Him. He just asks us to obey....again. So, getting back to baptism, when we submit to baptism it's like saying, "Ok, God, I'm ready to do this the right way. You have set our relationship straight by paying the price for my sin. I love You so much and I want to prove I love You so I'll do whatever You ask."

Perhaps, (or more than likely), there are deeper, more theological reasons to believer's baptism. This is just the way that I perceived it.

Mark wasn't ready for that. He liked his life the way it was. He despised getting up in front of a group of people, much less speaking in front of them. There was no way he was getting baptized. That in and of itself may not seem like a big deal but there were repercussions to his decision. His defiance actually made him more angry about things he'd hear in church. It started to get under his skin, so to speak.

Before I keep going on about Mark, I want to set the record straight that I was no saint. My motives may have been right in that I wanted our family to serve and live for God as a unified component. However, the sin of spiritual pride captivated my heart which caused me to sin against Mark. My communication to my husband was often laced with whining, yelling, berating and nagging. I didn't just resign my criticism to spiritual matters. I attacked Mark's parenting skills, his financial decisions, his hobbies, his motives which I felt I knew so well, acting like I could read his mind. My arrogance (thinking I was holier or better than Mark, especially concerning my relationship with God) just caused division between us. As the animosity between us grew, I found myself in tears more often than not. The cycle was always the same.   Mark would do something I deemed unacceptable, I would try to be "nice" and keep quiet, it would continue until I couldn't take it any longer and I would explode in anger, saying things I'd regret later then I'd cry for hours feeling like it was all hopeless.

It was during this period that Mark decided he didn't want any more children.   Chris was three months old and Mark hated the crying (of baby and wife) and the responsibility of raising a child.   My reproaching him as a parent didn't help matters. He went to see a doctor about getting a vasectomy. The doctor gave Mark some consent forms which I had to sign as well so I can't say it was only his decision.   I remember thinking I was probably going to divorce Mark anyway so I didn't care. After the surgery the doctor showed Mark the segment of vas deferens that he removed, indicating that it was more than the usual length and stated adamantly that it would never grow back. We never had to worry about having any more children together.

The Way He Teaches Me 3

1. God often allows me to go through a desert experience to prepare me for my greater purpose.

2. If I love God, I show Him by being obedient to His commands.

Chapter Four

2 CHRONICLES 16:9

What good is it, my brothers and sisters, if someone claims to have faith but does not have works? Can this kind of faith save him?
(James 2:14 NET)

Marriage was not working for me. Mark and I just couldn't get along. He had stopped going to church. I attended sporadically. I felt overwhelmed with being a mother, working part time, keeping house AND trying to be a good wife. Many times I contemplated how I could get out of it all. I couldn't afford to live on my own, with a baby. There seemed to be no answer.

Eventually I turned to God for the solution. When I was a new Christ-follower, one of my mentors, Phyllis, expounded on the idea that there is a battle that goes on inside each Christian. It's the battle between the flesh and the spirit...in other words, between what I want and what God wants. The flesh wants to do things that gratify the flesh, my self-interest. The spirit wants to do things that would gratify the Holy Spirit, and glorify Jesus. In this case my flesh wanted to do things like lash out in anger, belittle and berate Mark, and control him. The Spirit wanted me to love unconditionally, put Mark's needs before my own, and practice being patient and kind. This battle is real and happens every day in a Christian's life. Phyllis said it's like two lions in mortal combat. The lion that is fed the most will be the winner. I realized that my flesh gets fed automatically through my selfish desires within and from all the external temptations of the world such as secular media. Back then we didn't have the internet but the radio and television offered much to feed my fleshly nature. My spirit on the other hand, was starving. So as I turned to God for my solution, I decided I better start feeding my spirit.

I made the conscious effort to go to church regularly whether Mark went or not. I also joined a women's Bible study that met every week in a home that was a thirty minute drive from my home. It was an intense Bible study with much homework. God started opening my mind to His truth. I found that much of my beliefs did not line up with His truth. I started changing my way of thinking to line up with what the Bible said especially about marriage and love.

Somehow I started to see how blessed I was even in my difficulties. We lived in a beautiful lake community. Our son was a beautiful baby, growing healthy and strong. I loved my house, mostly because I never dreamed I'd ever be able to have one. One day, as I contemplated all the blessings I enjoyed, I thought of all the times I messed up; all the times I let my anger, pride or frustration get the best of me, hurting those around me. I cried to God, "Why do You bless me so much? I mess up so badly."

A little while later I received an answer. When I sat down to do some Bible reading I picked up where I had left off the last time I read it, in 2 Chronicles 16. I read through the chapter, stopping after I read verse nine. I reread the first part of the verse:

> For the eyes of the Lord move to and fro throughout the earth that He may strongly support those whose heart is completely His. (NASB)

As I read I heard the Lord speak to me inside my thoughts. He said, "This is why I bless you. You just keep working on making your heart completely Mine and I'll take care of the rest."

I was taken aback by the clarity of this message that I somehow confidently knew was from God. I had a peaceful assurance that everything was all right.

From then on I concentrated on making my heart completely God's though I wasn't sure what that entailed.

As I continued studying the Bible it really became God's word or message to me. Certain verses would seem to jump off the page at me because they so clearly pertained to situations I was finding myself in.

For instance, there was a time when a relative of mine really didn't care for me. To say they hated my guts is an understatement. I received harassing phone calls several times a day. Sometimes it was just a hang-up call. Other times it was a threat to do me bodily harm. The voice was unidentifiable so I could not prove it was this relative or an accomplice. I received anonymous letters filled with hatred. One time I received a small candle in the form of a witch with a note that said, "Go back where you came from, witch!" With the postpartum depression, the stress from this harassment caused more upheaval in my life than I thought I could handle.

One day as I was reading my Bible I came across a familiar, yet at the time, inconvenient passage.

> "You have heard that it was said, 'An eye for an eye, and a tooth for a tooth.' But I say to you, do not resist an evil person; but whoever slaps you on your right cheek, turn the other to him also. If anyone wants to sue you and take your shirt, let him have your coat also. Whoever forces you to go one mile, go with him two. Give to him who asks of you, and do not turn away from him who wants to borrow from you. You have heard that it was said, 'You shall love your neighbor

and hate your enemy.' But I say to you, love your enemies and pray for those who persecute you, so that you may be sons of your Father who is in heaven;" (Matt 5:38-45 NASB)

I sat there in utter dismay. Did God really mean this? I just couldn't believe that I was supposed to love someone who so blatantly hated me. They wanted me gone, out of their life, not loving them. I just shut my Bible and decided to go on as if I hadn't read it. However, God didn't let me off the hook. I remember clearly when God spoke to me again. I was driving a bus full of high school soccer players. The Lord said, "Remember that hate-mail you have been receiving? I want you to send love-mail. I want you to send flowers. I want you to send them anonymously, so that no one, including yourself, will have feelings of 'Holier than thou' or anything of the sort."

Right! That was the craziest idea I had ever heard. If I hadn't been surrounded by a bunch of high school athletes I probably would have exclaimed "You've got to be kidding me!" Not only did I not want to love my enemy, I didn't have two dimes to rub together and sending flowers was way out of my budget. I didn't want any part of this.

I tried to ignore God and just move on but I couldn't. My Mom used to say that one of the things she liked best about me is that when we would have a disagreement I would go up to my room and contemplate the problem for a while then come downstairs and apologize. I did the same thing with God. Eventually I gave in and did as He wanted. I scraped together some money and sent flowers.

This was one of my first lessons in learning to obey God quickly. He doesn't let up until I do obey anyway so I better just get it over with. I also learned that doing what God asks of me doesn't mean that everything automatically turns out happily ever after. Nothing changed with my relative until years later. To this day I don't know if they ever realized the flowers were from me. I do know God's Word never fails. I was the one who changed. My heart eventually grew to love them. Today I have a very nice relationship with this person and I'm very grateful I didn't react the way I wanted to because that would have alienated us from each other forever.   Love and forgiveness trumps bitterness and revenge.

I think the area in which I had the most difficulty learning to do things God's way was in my marriage. I grew up in a family with a long ancestral line of strong-willed women. Being a strong woman in today's society is viewed as becoming and essential, but being strong willed in marriage can often display itself as bossy, nagging and obnoxious. When I was right, and I knew I was right, I could argue and talk-down Perry Mason himself!   (Showing my age here) And if that didn't work I could throw a tantrum better than any two-year old in the candy aisle. Mark and I were both the first born children in our families, used to wanting things our own way. We butted heads quite often. God had His work cut out for Him!

One time after a horrific argument with Mark had left me in tears and consternation I telephoned my friend Margaret, the one with whom I shared the hospital room when our babies were born. As I poured my heart out in deep grief and pain there was only one thing she would reply to each complaint, "Well, you know you can't get divorced." She repeated it over and over and I really didn't want to hear that. I guess I was hoping if I came up with a complaint bad enough she would finally change her tune. She didn't and today I have to say I am glad for that. She had the Biblical mindset that "What

God has joined together, no man can separate." I didn't understand it at the time but my marriage *was* put together by God. Many would look at our situation and say we were together only because we "had" to get married but I now see it differently. God creates babies. There are no accidents in His creation. There were times I could have become pregnant with someone else and yet Mark was the one God chose to be the father of my baby. Twenty-nine years later I know with all my heart that was no accident. Thankfully I listened to Margaret and stayed with Mark.

One of the first steps towards salvation for my marriage was a Bible study by Kay Arthur called "Marriage Without Regrets". I faithfully labored through the homework and attended the group meetings once a week. Some of the lessons I learned about God's perspective on marriage were so contrary to what I had grown up believing.

For instance, God's idea about sex and mine were worlds apart. I was a teenager in the 70's and we were told "if it feels good, do it." Sex wasn't something saved for marriage, it was meant for that "special someone" or even just for fun. Today it's even more of a pastime, along the same lines as watching TV or playing golf. I learned in the Bible study that God actually created sex. However He had some rules. I always thought it was something I'd sort of hide from God (like I could). I learned that it was something to be enjoyed between a man and a woman, who were married. It was a wonderful wedding gift they were to give to each other. It's really rather intriguing if you think about it. If sex is just something one does with anyone, what's so special about being married? Sex is the only thing in the world that I can do with my husband that I can't do with anyone else. I can hug someone else, even kiss another, platonically. But sex is something very special that God has reserved for those who make a commitment to each other in marriage.

"Marriage is to be held in honor among all, and the marriage bed is to be undefiled; for fornicators and adulterers God will judge." (Hebrews 13:4 NASB)

My son told me that when other teens thought he was crazy for not having sex yet at his age, which was probably around sixteen, he explained it to them this way: What if I have sex with all these different girls and then finally I find the one girl that I'm going to marry. She's the perfect match for me in every way except she's not as good at sex as one of the other girlfriends. That's going to be detrimental to our relationship. If I never had sex before I wouldn't have anyone to compare her with.

As it turned out, he did keep his virginity until he was married. He married a beautiful young woman perfectly matched for him. His wedding night truly was a gift from God.

As I continued to study "Marriage without Regrets" I learned that men and women have different needs, both physically and emotionally. I learned that my husband was never meant to be exactly like me, no matter how much I wanted him to be. We, men and women, are created in such a way that together we make a complete picture. Communications, emotions, ideas, thought patterns are different and need to be understood as such. There are so many superb books which I have listed at the end of this book that have helped me discover the keys to all that makes a relationship between husband and wife work the way God intended. These are books that I have read over twenty-eight years and continue to read to keep my heart and mind going in the right direction. I didn't change over night. I am so thankful, however, that looking back now I do see that I did change and to me that is a miracle.

Living with a man who was used to doing what he wanted, when he wanted and didn't see the need to take into consideration how it would affect his wife or child caused me great mental turmoil. I had five younger siblings and I often had to care for them. Being responsible came naturally to me. Mark was still enjoying his "glory years". Having a baby wasn't going to change anything for him.

One of the activities he still enjoyed was going out and drinking with his friends. Sometimes he wouldn't come home until hours past midnight. One such night, as I cried out to God about my situation, I picked up one of the books I had on my shelf and read it until 3 a.m.. I think the book was Love Must Be Tough by James Dobson. I was amazed when the author discussed going through the very same situation I was going through. God had led me to pick up the perfect book. It explained exactly how to react to someone who is not acting lovingly in a marriage. I decided to try his advice on Mark.

When Mark came home at 7:30a.m. I met him at the door and said, "Mark, I still love you. I don't know if you still love me, but when you love someone you don't treat them like this. If you ever do this again I just want you to know that Chris and I won't be here when you get home." I calmly turned around and went upstairs. It was a holiday, perhaps Mother's Day or Easter, which we normally went to my grandparents' house. He never enjoyed family get-togethers usually putting up a fuss about going. As I was getting ready Mark took a shower, got dressed and ended up going with us without a peep of complaint. I was amazed. Later he told me he was so surprised that I didn't scream at him as I normally would he knew he was in big trouble. The best part is he never did do it again! God's way really works.

As I was learning to be a "Godly wife" I knew that getting angry was not a Christian quality. I tried very earnestly to stay quiet and peaceful. What I didn't realize was that I was not dealing with my anger. I was stuffing it. It was smoldering deep down inside of me and eventually, when I "couldn't take it any more", I would blow up! I would dump it all on Mark and what a mess it would be. This cycle seemed never ending until I learned in the marriage Bible study that instead of stuffing or dumping I should give my emotions to God. I'm not sure what that meant to others but for me I decided to write out my frustrations to God in a journal. I just recently found those first journals I kept at the beginning of our marriage. The first few pages are filled with my angry thoughts toward Mark. I have no idea what he did as I didn't go into detail about his "faults" thankfully, but I see a pattern of frustration: crying out to God and then relief. In one entry after a few paragraphs of ranting I wrote, "Ok, God, I feel a little better, now. I'll try and trust...But it's so hard to trust when I hurt. I have never learned to do that. Maybe that's part of the lesson to be learned". In another entry I wrote "Now, to sort out my feelings. I think what You want me to learn is I am placing too much significance on this marriage. I am living for Mark instead of living for You. If You could only help me remember that 'My Maker is my husband', (Isaiah 54:5) that would take a lot of the pressure off. I have to remember -- You are my source of satisfaction, You are my provider, You love me, You understand me. No one, not even Mark, can do that."

I was beginning to understand what it meant to make my heart completely His.

The Way He Teaches Me 4

1. I concentrate on making my heart completely God's; He will strongly support me in everything else.

2. To make my heart completely God's, I have to know God's heart. The Bible is where I get to know His heart.

3. God's Word gives clear and perfect direction.

Chapter Five

CHANGING

"Lord, I crawled across the barrenness to you with my empty cup uncertain in asking any small drop of refreshment. If only I had known you better I'd have come running with a bucket."
~Nancy Spiegelberg

The battle of the lions continued to rage inside of me. I wanted desperately to let Jesus be the ruler of my life but it was so difficult. I had spent so much time over the years feeding my fleshly desires I believed it would be impossible for me ever to be what God wanted. I had to get more serious about feeding my spirit. I read in Ephesians,

> "You were taught with reference to your former way of life to lay aside the old man who is being corrupted in accordance with deceitful desires, to be renewed in the spirit of your mind, and to put on the new man who has been created in God's image – in righteousness and holiness that comes from truth." (Ephesians 4:22-24 NET)

These verses showed that this was something in which I had to be proactive. It didn't just mystically happen. *I* had to be the one making new choices and changing my "old man" by putting on the "new man". This verse says I had to be "renewed in the spirit of my mind." There were several ways in which I learned to do this.

I loved music. I was raised with my grandfather singing in a Barbershop chorus. I loved the perfect pitch and harmonies in their songs. My mother always had a "song for every occasion" as she called it. No matter what we were doing she had a song to go along with it. If she were washing my hair she'd sing "Gonna Wash that Man Right Out of My Hair", while cleaning our rooms it was just "A Spoonful of Sugar", and while tucking me in at night she'd sing, "Goodnight My Someone, Goodnight My Love", to name a few.   As a teenager I listened to all the popular songs on the radio. As a young adult the songs influenced my moods and my behavior. For instance, one time I got extremely intoxicated on a particular brand of alcohol because a song I liked on the radio glorified the liquor. Once I realized that music had such an effect on me I decided to listen to music that was more edifying, feeding my spirit rather than my flesh.

At the beginning of my life with Jesus I was introduced to a Contemporary Christian Music (CCM) artist named Keith Green.   As I listened to his albums I learned God's Word without really trying too hard.   His songs were filled with Biblical truth.   The lyrics seemed to resonate with my thoughts as if Keith were right inside of my head when he wrote them. I remember how blatantly some of the lines in the songs demolished ideologies I had learned as a child. This was so astounding to me, as the religion I was raised in was not one of the most popular nor was it's theology.   It wasn't until 20 years later while reading Melody Green's book No Compromise that I learned Keith was raised in the same religion as I.   My Heavenly Father loves me so much that He orchestrated details of my life to make sure I had music handed to me early in my relationship with Him that would speak to me clearly and distinctly to teach me His truth.

I loved Keith Green's music, and the other CCM music I could get my hands on, but at the time there was not a CCM radio station available. I couldn't afford to buy new albums all the time. To change my music listening habits was no easy task. I had heard about a CCM radio program which aired every Saturday morning for a few hours. Called "The David and Goliath Show", it broadcasted from Upsala College in East Orange, NJ. The host was George Flores, a young husband and father of six, who now DJs on the large local Christian radio station. Those few hours on Saturday morning were like my IV drip of hydration after a long thirsty week without Christian music. Eventually I recorded the Saturday morning show and listened to it over and over throughout the week.

Music wasn't the only area I realized I needed to change. The Bible teaches a principle illustrating that we take on the character of those with whom we associate. In Proverbs we read:

> He who walks with wise men will be wise, But the companion of fools will suffer harm. (Proverbs 13:20 NASB)

I took this to heart and sought out friendships with women that I "wanted to be like when I grew up". One such woman, Carrol, taught me to memorize scripture, use it in prayer, and study the Bible like I never did before. She and her husband, Paul, took Mark and me under their wings. They didn't just talk the talk...they LIVED Jesus out in front of us. The mercy and grace they extended to us in our foolish youthful years gave us inspiration and a Godly example to follow. Paul was the only man who treated Mark as, and called him, a brother in Christ, even though our immaturity in Christ was quite evident. Mark flourished under his tutelage. After Paul and Carrol moved away there were others that God put in our lives, men and women in and through whom we saw Christ living. I cherish their friendships, knowing that each enriched our lives and helped us become more conformed to the image of Christ (Romans 8:29), which should be the goal of every Christian. I continue to gravitate towards the more spiritually mature Christian ladies in church. I still want to be in the right company.

The Lord has given me my own "inner circle", lifelong friends in whom I can confide and on whom I rely to pray, support and challenge me when I need it. Julie, Lori, Lynn and

Diane have stood by my side through thick and thin and loved me in spite of myself. Even though I don't see them often, when we get the chance to get together, the Lord fills us with joy and we pick up as if time never existed. At some of my lowest points, just knowing I have these soul mates encouraged and strengthened my heart.

The most important change in my mind, in order to feed the right lion, came when I realized I had to make studying the Bible a priority. John Wesley, the 18th century preacher and co-founder of the Methodist Church, said, "God himself has condescended to teach me the way. He has written it down in a book. Oh, give me that book! At any price give me the book of God. Let me be a man of one book." I wanted to become a woman of one book. I read it as much as I could, taking notes and writing favorite verses on index cards in order to memorize them. I joined ladies' Bible studies. Chris was a baby so I went to those that had childcare available. The Christian radio stations, all TWO of them, were mostly "talk radio" back then. I had one or the other turned on as much as possible. I heard sermons and teaching by Biblically sound preachers. These were teachings that wrenched at the sin in my heart, and taught me the truth of God's love, grace and judgment, unlike those prevalent on TV and the radio today who preach, "let's all love Jesus because He wants to make us happy." What they forget to tell is that Jesus said, "If you love me you will obey My commands." That's where the heart wrenching comes in. However, I have found that after the wrenching there is a peace and joy that really surpasses all my understanding. I have also learned that doing things God's way has a much greater payoff than anything I could come up with in my own selfish desires for my life.

Changing human, self-centered behavior doesn't come easily nor does it happen instantly, but as I made those first changes in my life, my music, my friends and my Bible study, the leeches started coming off, one by one. I have to make it clear, however, that I didn't change myself.   It wasn't because I read so many self-help books, though those were influential, or I willed my heart to change somehow.   No, it was God, the One who told me, "You just keep working on making your heart completely Mine and I'll take care of the rest." I do my part, He does His.

One of my favorite instances of God doing a great work in me occurred in 1989. The Baptist church we attended had a Sunday evening service, along with the morning services. One Sunday afternoon I kept thinking about going to the evening service.   I didn't want to go.   I wrestled with the thought of going or not going.   Finally, I gave in and went. The speaker was a visiting missionary.   He was preaching from the scripture that many missionaries use as a call into mission work, Isaiah 6. As he read, I knew he was working up to verse 8 which reads,

> "Also I heard the voice of the Lord, saying, Whom shall I send, and who will go for us? Then said I, Here am I; send me." (Isaiah 6:8 KJV)

However, as he read verse 5, the heart wrenching began. He read,

> "Then said I, Woe is me! for I am undone; because I am a man of unclean lips, and I dwell in the midst of a people of unclean lips: for mine eyes have seen the King, the Lord of hosts. (Isaiah 6:5 KJV)

The wrenching began because I was suddenly very aware that I was a woman of unclean lips.   I don't think Isaiah's unclean lips were in the same rank as mine, which was vile and just profane. He was just so humbled by the presence of God he felt worthless and unclean, even though he was one of the most righteous men on earth at the time.   I could in no way equate my situation with his. I still had lots of leeches God was trying to detach. He was using this verse to break one free.

For some background information I was born in the 60's and my parents were teens in the 50's. In my mind my mom was the typical 50's girl, prim and proper. While raising her six children she never used harsh profanity. Once in a blue-moon a "damn" or "hell" would escape her lips but when that occurred I knew something really, really awful had transpired. My dad was a different story. I don't remember him using profane words often when I was younger, though my mother says he did. However, by the time I was a teenager, walking around my house was like going to an R-rated movie every day. For some reason I remember exactly when I inherited his "unclean lips". I was in middle school and I was walking with my friend up the hill towards school. I remember using every four letter word I ever heard as I was angry about something or other, the reason escaping my memory though the anger remains a clear recollection like it took place yesterday. To this day I feel so sorry for my sweet, clean-cut friend for having to listen to my tirade. From that time on, I was the walking R-rated movie character.

As I listened to the preacher that Sunday night in 1989 I cited in my mind many of the instances of profanity that crossed my lips. Tears pooled in the corners of my eyes, blurring my vision of the preacher as he finished his sermon. They streamed down my face as he gave the altar call to those who felt led to go into the mission field. No one answered that call, however, I did stand up and go forward, tears still flowing. I suppose everyone thought the Holy Spirit had been moving so on my heart to become a missionary that I was overwhelmed to tears. I quietly explained my situation to the preacher and my pastor and the latter did something I never saw him do before. He told the congregation about the conviction of sin God had placed on my heart and asked everyone to come forward and "lay hands" on me and pray for me to be delivered from unclean lips. It was a precious time of prayer, with different people praying for me. I felt so blessed and once again, I felt this lifting of a burden off my shoulders, as I had at my conversion. Some people came up to me afterwards and shared how God had helped them change the "words of their mouth," encouraging me to stay in the Word, and trust God to do a good work in me.

As I drove home I was worried I would fail. It had been a bad habit and I didn't think there was any way I could just stop cursing. I had tried many times before but it seemed to be such a strong-hold in my life. However day after day following that Sunday evening service I prevailed without a profane word slipping past my lips. I was astonished and now, so many years later, I see God really had delivered me from "unclean lips".

Unfortunately, I can't say I *never* uttered profanity again. I have found that when I haven't fed my "spiritual lion" and I'm walking the "fleshly" one, an expletive will slip out in extremely adverse situations. However, there is a difference. Before that church service in 1989 I couldn't control my tongue at all. Now, even when words slip out that I regret later, I know I had a choice. Every time it has happened I had been in a state of frustration. It's been said that frustration is a fruit of the flesh. The Bible says the fruit of the Spirit is love, joy, peace, patience, kindness, goodness, faithfulness, gentleness and self-control. (Galatians 5:22) I have learned that if I pay attention to my feelings when I start getting frustrated, I can stop myself and pray, "Lord, let Your Holy Spirit take over right now so that I don't continue walking in my flesh." Usually, that's all it takes. I start to feel peace and change my line of thinking about the situation.

For instance, let's say I'm behind schedule, trying to get out of the house to Bible study. The dog threw up in the living room and I just burnt the biscuits. I know that frustrated feeling. It starts down in the depths of my belly. If I stay in that state and one more thing happens...#@&%! That's all it takes. However, there have been times when I have turned the situation around by remembering that frustration is a fruit of the flesh. Paul wrote,

> "But I say, walk by the Spirit, and you will not carry out the desire of the flesh." (Galatians 5:16 NASB)

As I've asked the Holy Spirit to control my thinking I've calmed down and remained in control of my tongue. Then the Spirit takes over and He prevails.

Change doesn't come easy to most people. We have to get out of our comfort zones -- do things against our natural desires or tendencies. Sometimes the Lord will tell us to do something that is so totally opposite of what the rest of the world thinks is right and we know we are going to pay a social price. Though those times are not always enjoyable at the outset, the ultimate conclusion is worth it all.

The Way He Teaches Me 5

1. I have to be proactive in putting on the "new man".

2. I have to renew my mind with God's Word and His ways.

3. I do my part, but God does the changing.

Chapter Six

HEARING

My sheep hear My voice, and I know them, and they follow Me
~ Jesus

Near the end of the last chapter I made a

statement about the Lord telling us to do something. Many people have asked me how I know when I am hearing God tell me anything. Some people think I'm pretty presumptuous to claim God told me something. To be honest when it happens, I too wonder if I am really hearing from the Lord. To me the first evidence that I am hearing from the Lord is this incredible peace that pervades my whole being. I usually ask, "God, is this really from You?" and I just sense His peace. The second way I know I'm hearing from God is, as they say, "the proof of the pudding is in the eating." As I've experienced this relationship with my Heavenly Father I have seen over and over again that I was hearing Him even at times when I wasn't sure it was Him that was speaking to me. The following stories are examples of times I have felt that I heard from the Lord and reciprocated to His leading. The results showed me that God was involved, one way or another.

One of the most absurd conversations I remember having with God occurred while I was potty training our son. Chris was just on the verge of being totally trained. This particular day he had been constipated for a couple of days. (I'm not sure it is proper to put "God" and "constipated" in the same paragraph but I don't know any better way to explain the situation so forgive me.) I gave him some prune juice. He really liked it and drank about three glasses. I then got worried and buckled him into his little wooden potty seat. I told him he couldn't get up until he "went". He sat there...and sat there...and sat there. I ran to the laundry room for a minute to throw a load in the washer, fretting and complaining and finally praying as I went. I remember telling God, "What am I going to do? I can't put him in a diaper. After all the prune juice he's bound to explode and then what a mess I'll have to clean up," and clear as day I heard the Lord say, "And then you'll know a little of how I feel when I have to clean up my children's messes." I was taken aback by this "thought" and the peace that just overcame me at the same time. I was really humbled by it and went upstairs with a renewed love for my baby and a little understanding of how God loves me...even willing to clean up my messes so I can have the life He created me for. I was going to let my son loose from the bondage of the potty chair, no matter what the cost would be to me, in a way like the Lord when He freed me from sin's punishment by taking it on Himself. However when I got there I found that he had done his duty! I was so thankful. In this instance I learned that God communicates to me in a variety of circumstances and situations.

That was an instance when I heard the Lord say something to me in my mind. I don't usually hear an audible voice. It's just like a thought, but somehow I know it's not my thought. I've learned that when God speaks to me it isn't like my own thinking, and as I wrote earlier, I usually argue with Him. Not that I really argue with God. It's more of a feeling of "Are you kidding me? Really?" and not "Oh, You are completely wrong, God."

There are other voices, or thoughts, that come into my mind that are not really mine. These are not as recognizable as God's. They come masqueraded as my own thoughts so I am often misled by them. Most of the time these thoughts have to do with my opinion of myself or something I have said or done. It's usually self-condemning and leads into a depressed state. These thoughts are not easy to combat. Too often I am overwhelmed by them and follow the downward spiraling path to which they lead.

I have learned that the content in these thoughts are not from God and therefore I need to evict them from my mind as quickly as possible. The way I know they are not from God is He never brings a condemning spirit over me. The Bible says,

> "There is therefore now no condemnation for those who are in Christ Jesus." (Romans 8:1 NET)

That does not mean God ignores my sin and bad habits. No, He's very concerned about my integrity and moral standing. However, when He wants to bring something to my attention it's more of a gentle yet firm admonishment. It reminds me of the youth leader I had when I was a teenager. One time, while we were on a retreat getting settled in for the night I got this bright idea to turn off all the lights in the cabin from the main breaker box. I wasn't alone in this prank but I probably instigated it. The curator of the retreat center happened to come in at that moment and was none too pleased. As he reported my misdemeanor to my leader I stood trembling. All my youth leader did was give me a look that said, "Dawna, I expect better of you." That was it. He assured the curator that it wouldn't happen again and of course, it didn't. I honored my leader so much that I wanted to make sure I never did anything that disappointed him again.

My relationship with God is a little like that. The Bible says we are to "fear the Lord". One aspect of a healthy fear of the Lord is to be afraid of displeasing Him because I love Him so much. So when God reveals something in my character that needs to change it's like He's giving me that "look". Then the wonderful outcome is that He has provided everything that I need to change.

> "If we confess our sins, He is faithful and just to forgive us our sins, and to cleanse us from all unrighteousness." (1 John 1:9 KJV)

My job is to confess, which means to agree with God that I have sinned, messed up, broken His laws. His promise is to forgive and then cleanse me. Sometimes the cleansing or changing happens quickly and other times it takes longer, maybe years, but I know God's promise, that He will cleanse me from all unrighteousness, will be fulfilled. The key is to keep listening.

As I stated before, I believe the "proof of the pudding" (that I'm hearing from God) "is in the eating," or in other words, if what I have heard actually works out in my life then I know it was from God. For instance, many years ago I saw a video at church about an alternative to Halloween called "Light the Night". This event would take place on Halloween, which due to it's connections to "the dark side" we had previously avoided altogether. The "Light the Night" event involved decorating the house with many lights, serving popcorn and playing games. I think it was intended for churches to do on their premises; however, I took the idea and made it into something I could do at home. We made it a time where we reached out to the neighbors, served hot apple cider, water, popcorn and other goodies, provided crafts for the kids and had the TV in the driveway playing Veggie Tales: Where's God When I'm Scared. We handed out Bibles and other Christian literature. The pièce de résistance was our "tomb stone" decorations. One would say: You can R.I.P. because Jesus Lives. Another said: Jesus Christ--This Grave is Empty. Every year it became bigger and better. I would pray and ask God what we should do. Each year it was a huge success.

One year, 2008 to be precise, as I prayed I got the idea to do an obstacle course. The Lord provided people to help, others to donate the hay bales and food. We had prizes for the winners. Everything was set. Then a few days before Halloween we got a freak snowstorm. My entire yard was covered by a foot of snow. As Halloween approached the snow did not disappear. I prayed and asked the Lord if I was supposed to change my plans for the obstacle course. The answer I received was, "No, continue as planned." I was skeptical but I really felt that I was hearing from God so I kept on track with the plans. The morning of Halloween my yard still had snow in it. I kept thinking I must have been mistaken in what I thought I heard God say. Then by early afternoon, the snow was melting away. I thought, "Well, even if it melts it's going to be too wet to do anything that involves running and jumping in the grass." Still I heard that "still, small voice" say "Carry on as planned". By the time the kids came around "Trick or Treating" there was only one small section of snow by our mailbox, and the rest of the yard was dry and perfect for the main event: the obstacle course. Everyone had a wonderful time and I learned to listen and obey, once again.

A similar instance that also involved weather, was in 2004. I got the idea to have a block party. I had found that I knew so many of my neighbors but they didn't know each other. I decided a block party would be a great way to introduce them all to each other. We picked a date and it was set but then something happened that we had to change the date. So I prayed about which date would be the perfect choice. As it turned out the date that came to mind happened to be my birthday. I thought that was a silly idea but the idea was fixed in my mind like cement. I asked God if this was really the date He wanted and I had such a peace come over me, I knew it was His idea. So we made all the arrangements, getting permission to block off the side street, planning the food, fun and inviting the neighborhood families to gather all together. However, the weekend of the party, what was left of a hurricane that had done great damage in Florida

THE WAY HE LOVES ME

decided to stop off in New Jersey before petering out to nothing. It poured all Saturday night and into Sunday morning the day of the block party. We went to church and I asked the Lord if I should cancel. I got a clear, "No, carry on." As we drove home from church the skies opened up with downpours. I started to cry because I was sure that I wasn't hearing God correctly anymore. I figured I was just making up these thoughts. When we arrived home, once again, I prayed, "Should I cancel?" and I felt like I clearly heard, "No, prepare for the party." So we worked on getting things ready. By the time we were to take the tables and chairs outside, the rain had stopped. By the time the guests started arriving the sun was shining. By the time we were eating and playing games, the ground was totally dry. What a wonderful birthday gift! Everyone had a wonderful time and I learned once again, that my Father really does love to communicate with me.

This has also worked the other way, where I planned something and the Lord told me to change plans. Every year since we first hosted Light the Night in 2003 the weather had been perfect. In September 2009 I started planning for the event. I was getting some great ideas but as I was planning the Lord made it clear to me that I was to plan the entire event in the garage. Again, I was amazed at the clarity of the message in my mind so weeks before Halloween we cleaned out the garage and got it ready to put on an "indoor" event. As it turned out, that year it rained on Halloween. I don't mean a light rain, either. It poured all day. We had a lovely time in our garage with neighbors stopping by to get warmed up with hot apple cider and some crazy games.

After our 2010 Light the Night ended I felt the Lord telling me we were finished hosting the festivities on Halloween. That year we had made it the grandest affair so far. I thought perhaps I was just exhausted and it was wishful thinking that we didn't have to do it any longer. However, as 2011 progressed and October approached I prayed again, asking God whether we should put on the outreach or not. I got a clear, "No". I felt we were truly done. That year Halloween was canceled due to another snow storm. In 2012 it was canceled due to Hurricane Sandy.

These are examples when I truly have been listening to what God is trying to say to me. Unfortunately, there are more times than I care to admit, and more that I don't even know about, where I have not listened, not asked, and I go forward in my own ideas and ambitions. Many of these times I end up making mistakes which I have to rectify or I know that the outcome could have been so much better had I stopped and allowed God to lead.

Another way the Lord speaks to me, the most important and clear way, is through the Bible, the Holy Scriptures.

> "All Scripture is inspired by God and profitable for teaching, for reproof, for correction, for training in righteousness; so that the man of God may be adequate, equipped for every good work." (2 Timothy 3:16, 17 NASB)

To me, the most important aspect of scripture is that it explains who God is explicitly. Without the Bible people can fabricate all sorts of ideas about God. Keeping our definition of God confined to the limits of scripture keeps us out of false teaching and also reveals the Lord's nature and attributes to us. There are several names our God has revealed in scripture that describe His character and attributes. El Shaddai (God Almighty, Genesis 17:1), Jehovah Jireh (the Lord sees [to it], Genesis 22:14), Jehovah Shammah (the Lord is there, Ezekiel 48:35), Jehovah Shalom (the Lord is Peace, Judges 6:24), to name a few, bring clarity to God's personality.

Reading the Bible ranks highest among all my activities. Many times I'll be in a situation or quandary and the very next section of scripture I read not only pertains to, but gives specific direction or advice for, my circumstance.

One of the most memorable instances of this occurred a few years ago. At the time I was the head of the sound booth ministry at our church. It was a ministry I felt the Lord had given me by divine appointment. At this point a subtle doubt had crept into the back of my mind that because I was a woman I couldn't be the head of a ministry that included men. The feeling of doubt seemed to intensify while I was in the company of two particular men in the ministry. I thought perhaps they could do a much better job than I. This sentiment kept growing until one day I felt I could take it no longer. Therefore one Saturday morning I told my family that after breakfast I was going into my room to pray until God gave me an answer. I had to settle this so I knew for sure: Did God appoint me to be the head of the sound booth ministry or should I resign? I sat myself down in my comfortable chair where I do my Bible study and opened my Bible to the place where I had stopped reading the last time. I prayed first: Lord, I'm going to read my Bible for today then You and I are going to sit here until You speak to me and make it plain if You want me to be the head of the ministry or not.

I opened my Bible to the bookmark where I had finished the last time I had read which happened to be at Isaiah 41. Apparently years earlier I had written my name in one of the verses so as I came to the passage it read: ...

> "You are my servant, (Dawna), I have chosen you and not rejected you. Do not fear, for I am with you; Do not anxiously look about you, for I am your God. I will strengthen you, surely

> I will help you. Surely I will uphold you with My righteous right hand.
>
> Behold, all those who are angered at you will be shamed and dishonored; Those who contend with you will be as nothing, and will perish. You will seek those who quarrel with you, but will not find them. Those who war with you will be as nothing , and non-existent. For I am The Lord your God, who upholds your right hand. Who says to you, Do not fear, I will help you." (Isaiah 41:9b-13)

I sat in utter amazement as I read those verses. It was the exact answer to my question. I had my answer just from the Bible reading. I was filled with joy and assurance. I left my room confident I was fulfilling God's will for my life.

Unbeknownst to me one of the two men I referred to earlier had been going to the leadership of the church with complaints about my leadership. Apparently there were other issues between this man and the leadership and very shortly after I had my revelation from Isaiah 41 this man was asked to leave the church. I was told he had "slandered" against me and others. I was very surprised but then I understood that my feelings of inadequacy must have been emanating from this man's opinion of me, about which I didn't even know. I learned how important it is to strive to be in ministry with a pure heart, undefiled by a judgmental spirit.

As with any relationship, listening is an integral part of my relationship with my Father who loves me and wants to have fellowship with me. As I've shared these experiences I've indicated how I've heard rather quickly from the Lord. However, there have been times when I feel like my prayers are bouncing off the ceiling. I don't hear an answer at all. I feel empty and wonder if God has something against me. I search my heart and mind for anything that could hinder my relationship with Him. If I feel that there is nothing hindering my prayers then I know God is telling me to wait. More importantly, if the Lord isn't telling me anything at the moment, I am to remember to <u>keep doing the last thing I heard Him tell me to do.</u> I must trust and obey Him completely and in totality.

The Way He Teaches Me 6

1. As with any relationship, listening to God is vital to my relationship with Him

2. The Lord works out the details; I just listen and obey.

3. The Lord speaks to me in my spirit through my thoughts, and through the Bible.

4. If I don't hear God speaking anything new to me, I am to just keep doing the last thing I heard Him say to me.

Chapter Seven

AMY GRACE

"Amazing Grace! How sweet the sound!" ~ John Newton

"Do you believe the stories in the Bible as truth? Do you believe that God caused the Red Sea to part and the Israelites walked across on dry land? Do you believe that the same God is at work in your life and can make a baby where there is not supposed to be a baby?"

These were thoughts that came to me in 1991, as I was walking to the car to take Chris, then five years old, to school. It must have happened in a split second but I remember it today, twenty-two years later, like it just happened, and it seemed like a long drawn out conversation with the Lord. As I answered in the affirmative, I was overcome by a sense of complete trust and faith that God was going to give me another baby. I was thoroughly astonished, as I've previously written about our decision not to have any more children, taking measures to assure that we didn't.

The years went by and there was no baby. Throughout the time I'd pray about it, fret about it and sometimes, I even forgot about it. I didn't tell too many people what I felt the Lord had told me. It seemed crazy, but I knew! I just knew God was going to give us another child.

Over those years we moved out of state. We took up residence in Colorado, New Hampshire and Pennsylvania. Then, it happened. I remember in April of 1997, while attending the baby shower for my sister-in-law, I was holding my niece, Karianna, only one month old at the time. She was just so precious. As I held her, I remember thinking what a joy it would be to have a little girl of my own, just like her.

Chris was eleven years old at that time. We were homeschooling and had made some friends of the many homeschoolers at the church we attended. One family, the McMullens, had three boys, the oldest being Chris' age. They became our closest friends and we spent much time together.

One day we were on a field trip together, riding with all the kids in the McMullen mini-van. My friend, Melisa, was several months pregnant. I was under a lot of stress due to some extended family issues and I was also experiencing a touch of PMS. After a long drive in the van, the children were getting restless and rowdy. I jokingly told them they had better watch out because they were dealing with one pregnant woman and another PMSing and there was no telling what we might do. A week or so later, in a similar scenario, I said the same thing. Melisa turned to me and said, "Still?" I looked back, clueless to what she meant. She said, "Are you still PMSing?" And for the first time I realized that she was right? I never had regular cycles to begin with but this was a little odd. As we stopped at the store, she enticed me to buy a pregnancy test. I told her she was totally mistaken, but I appeased her anyway.

Plans had previously been made that I would be cooking dinner at Melisa's house to help her since she was so pregnant. Mark met us there after work. I didn't tell Mark I had bought a pregnancy test, knowing he would think I had lost my senses. After dinner, as the guys went off to talk about "man stuff", Melisa urged me to take the test. The type of test I used would show two lines for a positive result. I had never taken one before so I didn't know what to think, especially when a faint second line showed up. Melisa was convinced I was pregnant. I was dumbfounded. When we showed the guys, Mark was skeptical. Melisa and her husband persuaded us to go home and try another test in the morning.

I was totally dismayed, confused and excited, all at the same time. I didn't sleep well that night. I arose from bed at 5 a.m., dressed and drove to the "open-24-hours" store to purchase another test. When I got home I took the test immediately. This time there was no mistake. Two, big, bright, beautiful lines!

I was ecstatic! I ran in to tell Mark and he was very happy. Then he instantly fell back asleep. It was only 6:30 in the morning after all, so who could blame him? I sat in our spare room and praised God. I wrote in my journal. I called my mom. She's the only one I could get away with calling that early. I thought I was going to explode from joy!

As the pregnancy progressed, we encountered all the joys of expecting a baby as if it were for the first time. We thought about names. As we discussed girls' names I considered the name Grace. After all, God's grace was truly in operation here. We had decided in our human will to cut off any chance of having more children, a choice we later regretted. We deserved no more children. God's grace was giving us what we didn't deserve...which is the whole meaning of grace. Our baby girl had to be called Grace. Then I recalled the female name we had chosen if Chris had been a girl: Amy. Mark and I still felt drawn to that name. When we put them together they flowed like a stream in a peaceful forest: Amy Grace. As I said the name out loud it just resonated with my spirit and from that moment I was pretty convinced I was having a girl. The next day at church we sang Amazing Grace and I heard "Amy (Amazing) Grace". Then I was totally convinced.

In November I started to have severe "Braxton Hicks" contractions. My due date was January 12th. My doctor took precautions in case it was pre-term labor and I was hospitalized. I was put on this horrendous medicine that slowed everything down, including my talking, walking and thinking. I was very nervous, wondering what it was doing to my baby. After a few days, I prayed and felt I should ask the doctor some questions. I wasn't a very good patient, I am ashamed to admit. I told him, "I bet 100 years from now they will be saying, 'I can't believe they had pregnant mothers on that stuff back then." The doctor said, "Yes, well medicine isn't a perfect science." That's all I needed. I reminded him that George Washington died from the doctors "blood letting" him and I announced I wanted to go home.

Before I was allowed to leave the hospital I was required to see the neonatal unit. It was heartbreaking to see all the tiny babies, some whose heads weren't much bigger than tennis balls. The McCaughey septuplets had just been born, so the news was full of all the complications they were experiencing from being born two months early. I was undeterred.

The last requirement before I left the hospital was a more accurate ultrasound that showed every little detail of my baby, even down to her ovaries! No doubt about it now. We were going to have a baby girl. The beautiful detailed images reminded me of Psalm 139.

> For You formed my inward parts; You wove me in my mother's womb. I will give thanks to You, for I am fearfully and wonderfully made; Wonderful are Your works, And my soul knows it very well. My frame was not hidden from You, When I was made in secret, And skillfully wrought in the depths of the earth; Your eyes have seen my unformed substance; And in Your book were all written The days that were ordained for me, When as yet there was not one of them. (Psalms 139:13-16 NASB)

I did go home and our baby was not born early.

The last two months of the pregnancy were the most interesting. As the holidays approached I got this brilliant idea! Since I was having this miracle baby, and I was having early contractions, mild though they were, and our birthing center was in Bethlehem, PA, I was totally convinced that she would be born on Christmas Day. I was so sure of it that we told family we couldn't travel from Pennsylvania to New Jersey for the holidays. The three of us went out to eat at a Japanese restaurant. When I made the reservations I wondered why the guy hesitated when I asked if they still had room. We arrived to an empty restaurant, with one other couple. Who goes to a Japanese Restaurant in the Poconos for Christmas dinner????!!!!!! It was just like something out of A Christmas Story. I was so embarrassed. However, we had a nice meal, entertained by the rookie chef, who returned to the kitchen to great applause. Returning home, I felt dejected and disappointed, as I went to bed without having my baby. I didn't have even one Braxton Hicks contraction.

The New Year passed and still no baby.

Then, January 7th, it happened. I went into labor around 4 a.m.. We arrived at the birthing center by 5:30 a.m., followed by my mother and two of my dearest friends, Lynn and Diane. Amy Grace Renne arrived into this world at 8:34 a.m. weighing 7 lbs 7.5 oz and 20 inches long. She was all wrinkled up and precious, and as I noticed her tiny hands I commented, "She has such long fingers, she's going to be a piano player." (I have it on video for proof!) As many know, Amy has been blessed with the gift of music, showing exceptional ability on the piano as early as four years of age. God's goodness to us never ceases to amaze me.

Since we used the birthing center instead of the hospital we went home the same day. By 3 p.m. Mark, Chris, my mom, Amy and I were settled into our family room to rest and watch It's a Wonderful Life. And it truly was.

However, two days later Amy appeared too "yellow". I knew from Chris' birth experience that she probably had jaundice. We took her to the doctor the next day. As I sat there in the waiting room, a man sitting next to me, noticing how tiny she was, asked how old she was. When I said three days old he replied, "Oh! She was born on Christmas." I thought he was confusing her birthday with the 6th which I knew was "Little Christmas" or "Three Kings Day" in some cultures, so I reemphasized that she was born on the 7th.

He replied, "Yes, that is Orthodox Christmas."

As soon as he said those words I felt like the Holy Spirit chuckled in my heart, "Gotcha!"

I thought, "God, you always surprise me in wonderful ways!"

I wanted Amy born on Christmas. The Lord answered that request in the affirmative, but I didn't realize it until the moment He chose to reveal it to me. Every detail of that moment was choreographed in perfect rhythm by the Ultimate Designer of my life. I thought about the "odds" of that man sitting next to me at that perfect moment, asking the perfect question and having the perfect answer. I mean, how many people know that January 7th is Orthodox Christmas? Add to that the fact that I had chosen a "Family Practice" physician accidentally, instead of a pediatrician so I was actually in the "wrong" waiting room. Even Amy being born in a birthing center, which meant we went home the same day, and coming down with jaundice so I was obliged to take her to be examined, all part of the beautiful scheme laid out by my loving Father.

The Way He Teaches Me 7

1. God keeps His promises, even though we may have to wait a while.

2. The events of my life are expertly planned out by a perfect Designer.

3. God loves to reveal part of His plan to us, then work them out in ways that totally astound and amaze us, usually as something of which we never would have thought.

Chapter Eight

STORIES

"These things happened to them as examples and were written for our instruction, on whom the ends of the ages have come."

(1 Corinthians 10:11 NET)

My mother raised me on the stories in the Bible. She would read them to me before I went to bed or on a breezy summer afternoon sitting on a blanket in the backyard with my two younger brothers fidgeting beside me and my baby sister who was quietly playing with her toys.

I am the eldest of my mother's six children, and the only one she had with my father. They divorced when I was two years old, so we lived with my grandparents until my mom remarried when I was four years old. I was an only child for five years. My mom invested her love of the Bible into me during that time. Once my siblings came along our Bible-time grew less frequent but not less important. She gave me a good foundation in Biblical knowledge and practical application.

It seems that is what is missing in so many lives, even of those who claim to follow Christ: Practical application of the Bible's stories, principles and precepts into everyday experiences. Because of the way I was raised to me it's just the normal way to live.

When my mother would ask me what Bible story I wanted her to read to me I invariably answered, "Esther". I think I was attracted to the excitement, intrigue and ultimate "good overcomes evil" in the story. The main character, Esther, a girl from an obscure Jewish family, living under foreign rule, far from home, rises up to be the queen, who saves her people from destruction at the hand of an evil enemy, even at the risk of her own life. Though the name of the Lord is never mentioned, the story is replete with evidence of God's interaction in and sovereign control over Esther's life and the nation of Israel, as well. I love the fact that "Esther" is my sweet daughter-in-law's name. Once again I feel God's handiwork in my life, as this is another reminder that God is sovereignly directing my life and circumstances with his loving care.

My life has never been characterized as one of having great wealth. Financial wisdom did not run in my family. I didn't attend college. I never had high paying jobs nor has my husband. We have had to rely on God's mercy throughout our marriage and we have seen some wonderful demonstrations of His love and grace poured out on us over the years. There are so many passages of scripture that pertain to wealth, finances and daily sustenance. Some of my favorites are found in what we call Jesus' Sermon on the Mount found in the book of Matthew chapters five through seven.

In these following verses I learned a principle that would keep me trusting God even in the most dire of circumstances:

> "No one can serve two masters; for either he will hate the one and love the other, or he will be devoted to one and despise the other. You cannot serve God and wealth. "For this reason I say to you, do not be worried about your life, as to what you will eat or what you will drink; nor for your body, as to what you will put on. Is not life more than food, and the body more than clothing? Look at the birds of the air, that they do not sow, nor reap nor gather into

barns, and yet your heavenly Father feeds them. Are you not worth much more than they? And who of you by being worried can add a single hour to his life? And why are you worried about clothing? Observe how the lilies of the field grow; they do not toil nor do they spin, yet I say to you that not even Solomon in all his glory clothed himself like one of these. But if God so clothes the grass of the field, which is alive today and tomorrow is thrown into the furnace, will He not much more clothe you? You of little faith! Do not worry then, saying, 'What will we eat?' or 'What will we drink?' or 'What will we wear for clothing?' For the Gentiles eagerly seek all these things; for your heavenly Father knows that you need all these things. But seek first His kingdom and His righteousness, and all these things will be added to you. "So do not worry about tomorrow; for tomorrow will care for itself. Each day has enough trouble of its own. (Matthew 6:24-34 NASB)

These verses correspond with 2 Chronicles 16:9 indicating that if I put God and His Kingdom first He will take care of everything I need.

Sometimes these verses were specifically played out in my life. For instance the verses about clothing. I've never been a fashionista but I do like to dress nicely once in a while, especially for church.

About twenty years ago I was in need of some white dress shoes. I had a little money saved up for a pair but my search at stores that were within my budget availed nothing. Either they didn't have my size or there was nothing I found attractive. I remember stopping in the middle of one of the store-searches thinking about these verses and saying, "Ok, Father, You have promised to clothe me as well as you clothe the beautiful wildflowers. Please help me find some nice white shoes in my price-range, unless of course, I don't really need white shoes, in which case I trust Your better judgment."

I ended my shopping excursion empty handed but not downcast. I chose to trust my Heavenly Father's care for me and if I really needed white shoes, I would have them.

The following Sunday a friend at church asked me what size shoes I wore. When I told her she explained that she had been housekeeping for a wealthy woman who was disposing of some nice shoes. When she showed them to me I was amazed once again. Not only was there a beautiful pair of white leather flats, exactly what I was looking for, but also navy and brown pairs, all made of leather by expensive makers. I wore them for years. I have replaced the heels on the white pair once or twice and they have come back in style. As a matter of fact you will find my fifteen year old daughter, the fashion connoisseur, wearing them more often than I do these days.

Scripture has been the foundation of my life. I've studied, memorized and meditated on the Bible throughout my walk with Jesus and it's given me clear direction in many instances.

One time that I recall vividly took place when we lived in Colorado. The passage of scripture God used to direct our path was from Joshua.

Before I get to that part, let me give you the background story, which I have found remarkable every time I recollect it. We had been living in Colorado for about 18 months or so, but we felt we didn't belong there and we were supposed to move back east. However, we weren't in any position to make the move and it seemed extremely unlikely that we ever would.

On New Year's Eve my mother called to ask if I would be able to come back east for a week to help take care of the family business while she and my step-father went on a cruise. They would pay the airfare for Chris and myself to make the trip. I eagerly agreed and searched the internet for the best airfare. I had found a fare so low that my step-father jokingly asked if it were inside the plane. At that rate they offered to pay for Mark as well. Mark felt he would not be able to take the time off from work, but he wanted to go back home so badly that he proposed he would just call out sick. We both felt that would be the wrong thing to do but didn't know what else to do. We read in the Bible:

> "How blessed is the man who does not walk in the counsel of the wicked, Nor stand in the path of sinners, Nor sit in the seat of scoffers! But his delight is in the law of the Lord, And in His law he meditates day and night. He will be like a tree firmly planted by streams of water, Which yields its fruit in its season And its leaf does not wither; And in whatever he does, he prospers." (Psalms 1:1-3 NASB)

Proverbs 3:6 says

> "Seek His will in all you do and He will show you which path to take".

We had booked Mark's ticket after mine so he was on a different flight. As it turned out his flight got canceled due to the blizzard of '96 on the east coast. Chris and I were in New Jersey and Mark was stuck in Colorado.

Mark decided at last to do the right thing and asked his employer for time off, to which amazingly they consented. He arrived a day later than originally planned and we had a wonderful week of reunion with our family and friends.

Near the end of our stay we decided, very impromptu, to take a ride up to New Hampshire. A former co-worker of Mark's from the bus company in New Jersey, had moved there. He had contacted Mark several times while we lived in Colorado, encouraging Mark to come visit him. He had taken a bus driving job in Concord, NH. That was all we knew. We didn't even know the name of the bus company. We didn't have his phone number or address. We decided to check out the area and then maybe the next time he contacted Mark we could find out more information.

We arrived in New Hampshire very late so we stayed overnight in a motel. The next morning we followed the map and roadsigns to Concord. We had no cell-phones or GPSes in those days. As we drew closer to the city, the highway sign read "Concord: Next Three Exits". Mark asked me what we should do. I was always the navigator as he was the best driver! As we approached the first exit I felt like we should pass it. At the next exit I said, "Take this one." Driving down the road leading towards Concord was our only choice from that exit. We drove a short distance and Mark saw a bus company: Concord Trailways. He remarked that he was pretty sure that was the company his friend worked for. We kept driving and came to a stop light where we could only turn left or right. As we waited for the light to change, debating which way to turn, a Concord Trailways bus came from our left and turned right onto the road we were on, heading back to where we had just come from. Mark declared that it was his friend driving the bus! We assumed he was going back to the bus depot. We turned the car around, headed back to the bus depot and stopped to see if the driver was indeed who Mark thought it was. Mark left Chris and me in the car while he went inside the building to ask someone. It was pouring rain and all the snow from the blizzard was quickly being washed away.

It seemed like an eternity while we waited. Finally I decided to check and see what was taking so long. I quietly entered the building. It was a Saturday so there weren't many people around. As I approached closer to the voices of Mark and another man, I overheard the words, "if you want this job". I was startled and instantly turned around and went back to the car. When Mark returned he had an amazed look on his face. He told us that the driver we saw was indeed his friend but we had missed him by a minute as he was now driving to Boston. Then Mark proceeded to tell us that he had been offered a job by Concord Trailways. He could start in two weeks.

My mind started spinning. Maybe this was God's way of "ordering our steps" so that we could move back east. The drive back to New Jersey was filled with questions, discussion and wonder.

When my parents arrived back from their cruise we told them what had happened. My mom listened with an amazed expression. When I finished our story she replied, "The last person we met on the cruise was from New Hampshire. Maybe I could contact them and see if they know of a place Mark could stay." Mark would need an inexpensive place to reside temporarily if he took the job in two weeks, while Chris and I stayed in Colorado to sell the house.

As it turned out, she did contact them, and not only did they connect us with someone, it was a blessing beyond belief. The people had a place, right in Concord, two blocks from the bus company, that they wanted someone to stay in, look after, and do some work as they had moved to another residence which they were remodeling. Mark would be able to stay there rent-free.

Everything went as planned, Mark gave his notice and packed up the car to drive back east alone. Our house was listed with a realtor friend of ours and it was a sellers market. We should have the house sold quickly and Chris and I would join Mark in no time. As it turned out our house did not sell quickly. As a matter of fact, no one even came to look at it. We were stunned as it was priced very competitively.

I started to pray and seek God's answer to my dilemma. I was reminded of Joshua and the Israelites as they were finally about to enter into the land that God had promised them. In Joshua 3 we read,

"After three days the leaders went through the camp and commanded the people: 'When you see the ark of the covenant of the Lord your God being carried by the Levitical priests, you must leave here and walk behind it. But stay about three thousand feet behind it. Keep your distance so you can see which way you should go, for you have not traveled this way before.'" (Joshua 3:2- 4 NET) "After three days the leaders went through the camp So when the people left their tents to cross the Jordan, the priests carrying the ark of the covenant went ahead of them. When the ones carrying the ark reached the Jordan and the feet of the priests carrying the ark

> touched the surface of the water –
> (the Jordan is at flood stage all
> during harvest time) – the water
> coming downstream toward them
> stopped flowing. It piled up far
> upstream at Adam (the city near
> Zarethan); there was no water at all
> flowing to the sea of the Arabah (the
> Salt Sea). The people crossed the
> river opposite Jericho. The priests
> carrying the ark of the covenant of
> the Lord stood firmly on dry ground in
> the middle of the Jordan. All Israel
> crossed over on dry ground until the
> entire nation was on the other
> side." (Joshua 3:2, 14-17 NET)

As I meditated on these verses I realized that these priests had to step into the raging, flooding waters before God did His miracle which allowed them to walk across on dry ground. Previously, with Moses at the helm, God separated the waters first, then the people walked across. Dr. Martin Luther King, Jr is quoted as saying, "Faith is taking the first step even when you don't see the whole staircase." These folks didn't even see one stair-step!

As I prayed about my situation I felt the Lord leading me to go to New Hampshire and be with my husband, the family altogether, and God would take care of the house. I telephoned our realtor and asked him if it would be appropriate to pack up and leave the house empty, and what would it entail to sell the house while living in New Hampshire? He assured me that it was possible and done often. My friends and family thought it was a crazy idea. I should stay there until the house sold and I had the money in my hand.   However, I knew my right place was with my husband.

When I called my husband and discussed the idea with him, he was elated. He was so lonely and miserable by himself in a strange, new area.   That settled it! I told the realtor we were leaving as soon as possible.

Within one hour of making that decision, the phone started ringing with prospective buyers interested in the house. The final outcome was that our house sold for more than our listed price.   I learned once again that doing things God's way is way more effective...and far more entertaining.

The Way He Teaches Me 8

1. The Bible contains the practical advice for today's situations.

2. So faith comes from hearing, and hearing by the word of Christ. (Romans 10:17 NASB)

3. I can trust God's Word to work in my life in wonderful ways, never "returning void."

Chapter 9

FATHERS

"It is easier for a father to have children
than for children to have a real father."

(Pope John XXIII)

Being born in Tahoe, California sounds so exotic and glamorous. When people ask where I was born, and I respond with Tahoe, they get all starry-eyed and filled with astonishment. For me, it brings to mind the beginning of the long trail of broken relationships that my life would contain.

My mother had moved to California to relieve herself of a painful home life in New Jersey. She was twenty-one years old, legal and ready to fly the coop. Her sister had previously moved to the west coast and loved it, never to return to the east for her residence. My mother met and married my father within the first year of arriving in the Golden State. I was born eight months after the wedding.

Years later, my mother related the story of how the marriage grew troublesome almost immediately and by the time I was eighteen months old the two of them could barely stay in the same room together. As my mother recollected, when she informed my father that she wanted a divorce he got violent and hit her. As she was regaining consciousness she found herself being smothered with a comforter. She decided to pretend she had passed out again and she found he let her go. The next thing she knew he was gone and had taken me with him. He never came back.

The next few months my mother, three thousand miles away from her parents, worked frantically to find me and get me back. There were hearings, psychology tests and investigations. She turned to a religion she had been introduced to by some people for whom she had babysat when she was younger. This is the religion I was eventually raised and taught in, and to which she continues to adhere to this day. She credits it for getting her through this horrific time.

Finally, the judge told my father that if he didn't bring "the baby" back to the area by such and such a time on such and such a date, he would put my father in jail.   From my mother's side of the story, all she knew was, my father did as he was told and I was brought back, after several months of separation from my mother. After being away from her for months I didn't know my own mother and she had to coax me back into her arms. The judge advised her to take me as far away from my father as possible, because in his opinion that would be the best for everyone concerned. My mother did just that and for years we never knew the "rest of the story".

As I grew older and my mother relayed the story to me I never took to heart the part about my father being so aggressive. In my childhood mind my father was out there somewhere and he loved me and he was going to rescue me from the loneliness and pain I eventually suffered growing up in a troubled family.   However, he never appeared on the horizon of any part of my life.   The emptiness I felt from that never subsided.

When I was twenty-two, coincidentally the age of my mother when I was born, I took a road trip with a friend and ended up in the land of my beginnings--California. While staying with my aunt I looked up my father's name in the phone book. I knew the name of the town his family was from and I knew my grandfather's name, which is the name I found in the phone book. With anticipation and eagerness I dialed the number. A woman answered and I told her I was looking for my father and gave her his name. She asked who I was and when I replied, "This is his daughter, Dawna." All she could do was repeat my name, over and over. It was just like a scene from a dramatic movie.

When she recovered from the shock she sadly announced to me that my father had passed away many years before. When I explained where I was we made arrangements for a meeting with her and my aunt, my father's sister.

I traveled by bus from Sacramento to Manteca, not a short distance. I was met with open arms and loving embraces. During our lunch together we exchanged stories and memories and laughs. I learned that I had many of my father's features and characteristics. I also learned where I had been during those months twenty years before, while I was missing from my mother.

I recall dearly, as my grandmother, said, "I know someone who would love to hear from you--Aunt Cleeta and Uncle Bill." These were my father's aunt and uncle who lived in Colorado. As she dialed the phone number, I waited curiously. I was introduced quickly, and took the phone.

"Dawna, is that you?", the voice on the other end of the line asked.

"Yes?", I answered expectantly.

"We were just talking about you today." the woman replied.

I was dumbfounded. "Really?" I asked. How ironic! After twenty years, the day I happened to telephone, my great-aunt was talking to another relative and my name came up.

Then I heard the rest of the story. After my father had left my mother, taking me away, he arrived in Colorado at his aunt and uncle's home. They loved children and babysat several in their home. Their own son had passed on not too many years before, leaving them with their daughter as an only child.

My father had told them that my mother had become violent and was trying to kill me. He asked if he could leave me with them, that perhaps they could adopt me. Then he left. That was all these dear people knew. They took care of me, loving me, teaching me as if I were their own. They potty trained me. I also discovered I had the chicken pox while I was with them. I always wondered why I never got them the year my siblings and the rest of the neighborhood kids did. What a smile that brought to my face!

Then one day, they got a phone call. The man on the other end told them he was a lawyer from California. He informed them that if they brought me to a certain courthouse at a specific time they would be allowed to adopt me. My aunt and uncle immediately made the arrangements and arrived with me on time at the designated place. To their utter dismay, I was taken away from them, as they realized they had been brought there under false pretenses. All those years following, they assumed my mother had set up the entire scheme to get me back. If they had really thought about it, though, they should have realized that only one person knew where I was, and it wasn't my mother.

That was the day I learned that my father was a liar and a conniver. I learned that I really did have some of his characteristics. However, by God's grace I was learning to overcome them.

My aunt and uncle ended the phone conversation by telling me that they were Christians and they had been praying for me all these years. What a wild revelation! I was amazed at the way our Father in Heaven had allowed me to find the people who had prayed for me. He showed me that I probably had become a Christ-follower because of their prayers, and He had allowed them to see the answer to their prayers, even twenty years later.

The next "father" I had in my life was my grandfather. My mother took the judge's advice and transferred us back east to live with her parents. My grandparents poured out their affection on me. Grandpa was still working then and one of my favorite memories is when he would come home from work and sit in his easy chair with his martini and newspaper. I would stand behind the chair and comb his very few remaining hairs into an upward point. I never recall my grandfather raising his voice. Even when he was angry he remained soft spoken.

My grandfather was a hard worker, born in 1899, the eldest of five children. His father was an alcoholic and Grandpa would often engage employment throughout his teen years to help support his family. He was a no-nonsense type of a guy. He believed in working hard, provided for his family and retired comfortably. My grandfather was the most stable, moral man in my life. Unfortunately I didn't realize this when I was young, at times when I should have asked his advice or gained from his wisdom. Thankfully, we did have some precious time with each other near the end of his life. Watching the Yankee games together and sharing his love of Barbershop music will always remain my fondest of memories. His stories of life in the early part of the 20th century, kept me captivated.

The only thing I don't remember about my grandfather was him ever hugging me. He was never unloving, but he didn't express his affection as my grandmother did. She was always doting on me, as I was her first grandchild. Grandpa was always the hardworking provider. He was always there in the background. It wasn't until he was in his eighties that we developed a loving, bonding relationship.

When I was four years old I received my next father, as my mother remarried. After the wedding my step-father adopted me and I obtained a new name and a new life. We moved away from New Jersey to a suburb of Chicago. When I was five my first brother was born. Two years later my second brother was born. Eighteen months later my sister arrived. Soon after that we moved back to New Jersey. I was ten years old and devastated that I had to leave everything that was familiar to me.   As life unfolded in New Jersey I was more unhappy.   For years to follow I felt my parents had served me a great injustice and I never forgave them for leaving Illinois.   My adopted father, now the only "Dad" I knew, had left his secure employment to open his own business. Life got chaotic and stressful causing my parents to often argue severely.   Then my mom found out she was expecting again! It wasn't until she delivered them that she found she was carrying twins...my third and fourth brothers. I was eleven years old.

My mother always said, "If people knew to be better, they would be." I guess I could say that for my parents. They didn't have a clue how to raise six children in a world that was changing dramatically, and not for the better. Without getting into great detail at this point, I have to convey the idea that growing up with my dad left me hurt, angry and emotionally unstable.   As I matured into adulthood these attributes followed me.

For years I grieved over not having the "normal" father/ daughter relationship I saw my friends had.   Much later, when I read that a girl's relationship with her father is a determining factor in the relationships she chooses throughout her life, I cringed, understanding better that I followed suit when choosing boyfriends and spouses. Christian psychologists concluded that young women without a good paternal relationship were more likely to be promiscuous and rebellious, and unable to maintain good relationships with men. Dr. David Ireland writes, "The lack of self control is seen when a young lady becomes involved with the wrong man in hopes of filling a void created by an unloving father." I blamed my fathers for their mistakes that caused me such pain and I blamed my mother for choosing such lousy fathers for me. I lived in this grief for a while.

Eventually, through more study of the Bible, and learning that Jesus called His Father "Our" Father, I realized that my God was the best Dad I could ever have. I started addressing Him as "Daddy".   I called on Him whenever I had a problem...and He answered! I cried out to Him when I was hurting...and He comforted me.   He constantly provided everything I needed. On Father's Day, a day that used to be painful, I now wish My Daddy a Happy "Father's Day!" and find myself filled with great joy.

The most important lesson in my life is learning how my Father loves me. It's not been easy. I had been abandoned, ignored and abused by my human fathers. I have often read noted authors proclaiming the problem of people not understanding the love of God because they had such bad examples set by their human fathers. We relate the love of the Father to that imperfect relationship. I didn't think I had that problem because I had quickly learned that my Heavenly Father, who is different from my earthly fathers in every way, loves me unconditionally.   However, I have recently discovered that even though I know He loves me, I don't have that perfect trust in His sovereign plan and power in my life. Because I have been so disappointed by my earthly fathers, who claimed they loved me, I find myself discouraged and dejected when things don't turn out the way I think they should believing that my Father in Heaven is untrustworthy. As I wrap my mind around this I realize how irrational that line of thinking is. If the Creator of all things has taken time to reveal all these ways He loves me in the past, and has done such amazing things in my life, why can't I trust Him with the present and the future?

> "So do not be overly concerned about what you will eat and what you will drink, and do not worry about such things. For all the nations of the world pursue these things, and your Father knows that you need them. Instead, pursue his kingdom,

and these things will be given to you
as well." (Luke 12:29-31 NET)

Calling the Lord God Father is not something that is to be
taken lightly.   There is a misconception that all humans are
God's children.   The Bible says that God has only one
"begotten" son. Begotten comes from the word beget which
is defined as "(especially of a male parent) to procreate or
generate (offspring)".   Humans have not been begotten, but
created. Jesus is the only begotten Son, or child, of God.

However, the Bible does call people children of God.   So
how could that be? These verses help explain the process.

> "But as many as received Him, to
> them He gave the right to become
> children of God, even to those who
> believe in His name, who were born,
> not of blood nor of the will of the flesh
> nor of the will of man, but of
> God."   (John 1:12, 13)

> "Do everything without grumbling or
> arguing, so that you may (show
> yourselves to) be blameless and
> pure, children of God without
> blemish though you live in a crooked
> and perverse society, in which you
> shine as lights in the world by holding
> on to the word of life···" (Philippians
> 2:14-16 NET)

We see from these verses firstly that we are not
automatically offspring of God but may "become God's
children".   This is done, according to John, by receiving
Jesus, believing in His name. This would be called the "new
birth" which births us into God's family. Only through Jesus

Christ can this happen. In the verse above from the book of Philippians we learn that there is a differential between people groups. There are those that are "children of God, without blemish" and a society which is crooked and perverse. This implies that, again, not everyone is a child of God.

The new birth comes from repentance, the realization of sin and the turning away from it, and faith, trusting faith in the death, as penalty of sin, and resurrection of Jesus Christ. Only after this phenomenon do we have the right to be called "children of God".

There is another aspect to this concept. We, the children of God by faith, are not 'begotten", as Jesus was. Paul wrote,

> "For you have not received a spirit of slavery leading to fear again, but you have received a spirit of adoption as sons by which we cry out, 'Abba! Father!'" (Romans 8:15 NASB)

> He predestined us to adoption as sons through Jesus Christ to Himself, according to the kind intention of His will, (Ephesians 1:5 NASB)

> But when the fullness of the time came, God sent forth His Son, born of a woman, born under the Law, so that He might redeem those who were under the Law, that we might receive the adoption as sons. Because you are sons, God has sent forth the Spirit of His Son into our hearts, crying, "Abba! Father!" Therefore you are no longer a slave,

> but a son; and if a son, then an heir
> through God. (Galatians 4:4-7 NASB)

The Greek term υἱοθεσία (Huiothesia) was originally a legal technical term for adoption as a son with full rights of inheritance. (NET notes) Not only do we get to be called children of God, we receive all the benefits and rights of being in His family. Paul said we are "joint-heirs with Christ".

In my natural life, I was begotten by one man, and adopted by another. The one who adopted me made the choice to bring me into his life. God has done the same by choosing to adopt all who believe, trust and rely on His Son. I take that personally and feel overwhelmingly blessed that He has chosen to adopt me into His most amazing family, promising to love me with an everlasting love, which I can depend on no matter what may come my way. As every loving father lovingly gives gifts to his children, mine has given me the greatest gift. He has given me His Spirit to help me get through this life.

> "I will ask the Father, and He will give
> you another Helper, that He may be
> with you forever;" (John 14:16 NASB)

He has given me everything I need to be victorious. That is what a Good Father does

The Way He Teaches Me 9

1. God's sovereignty in my life includes the family I was born into. Even that He chose perfectly for me to be all He intended me to be.

2. When I trusted Christ as my Savior, I was adopted into His family and His Father became my Father

3. My Heavenly Father loves me perfectly, better than any earthly father could.

Chapter 10

TEMPTATION

"I have one good reason why you should walk
away from that temptation right now.
God. Is. Better."
~Francis Chan

When I first heard the lyrics to the song
Faithless Heart by Amy Grant on her Lead Me On album in
1988 I was dumbfounded. I felt I could have written them
myself. It was as if she had gotten inside of my mind and
captured my thoughts in rhyme. She described her feelings
of something missing in her marriage, thinking of another
who would romance her and give her the passion she longed
for. She fantasized about this stranger that would make
everything right. In the chorus she made the decision to tell
her faithless heart to leave and not come back. And
somehow...that helped me. It may have even saved my
marriage.

As a young girl I grew up with the "happily ever after" stories
of the lowly girl whose Prince Charming came to save her
from a life of misery. I had a vivid imagination and I had the
same recurring dream of marrying someone who cherished
me and treated me like a queen. After I married Mark and
found my husband fell far short of my imaginary Prince, I
often wondered if I had married the wrong man. I surmised
that my real soul-mate was out in the world somewhere and
one day we'd be together. I expected God to work out the
details. I had already determined in my heart that I couldn't
and wouldn't leave Mark, so He had to work it out...He just
had to.

When I heard Grant's song it resonated so much with my soul and emotions I realized that my feelings were not from God and they could not be trusted. I realized that if I wanted to have God's plan for marriage I had to work hard at *this* one, and learn to love my husband no matter what. It was not easy. Year after year married to a man that was so different from me in so many ways especially in our walks with God, I longed to escape, and often, in my mind, I did.

Eventually I had the revelation that these "mental affairs" were going to kill my marriage permanently, and it would be my own fault. I realized the fuel that fed these imaginations were the love-story type movies, the romance novels and even some of the "Christian" novels. I cut them out of my life. As much as I enjoyed them, I went cold-turkey. I started reading biographies and stories of Christian men and women who had served Christ with their lives. Some of my favorites include Bruchko, (Bruce Olsen) The Hiding Place, (Corrie Ten Boom) The Word Came with Power and biographies of George Mueller, Keith Green, Jim and Elisabeth Elliot and Fanny Crosby. I learned that these people were just that: people, real people, who made mistakes and were not perfect. The one thing they all had in common was they remained faithful to God, and their mates. They were trustworthy because they put their trust in Jesus, the "author and perfecter of faith". To be like that became my heart's desire. The psalmist wrote,

> "Delight yourself in the Lord; And He will give you the desires of your heart." (Psalms 37:4 NASB)

I learned the key to getting my heart's desire was to delight myself in the Lord. If the Lord is my delight then my heart will be full of His desires so I know they will be fulfilled.

It always came back to 2 Chronicles 16:9 and making my heart completely His so He could strongly support me. In this situation, dealing with my faithless heart, I needed ammunition to "crucify the flesh" as the Bible teaches in Galatians,

> "Now those who belong to Christ Jesus have crucified the flesh with its passions and desires." (Galatians 5:24 NASB)

I had learned that the Word of God is our Sword of the Spirit.

> "Finally, be strong in the Lord and in the strength of His might. Put on the full armor of God, so that you will be able to stand firm against the schemes of the devil. For our struggle is not against flesh and blood, but against the rulers, against the powers, against the world forces of this darkness, against the spiritual forces of wickedness in the heavenly places. Therefore, take up the full armor of God, so that you will be able to resist in the evil day, and having done everything, to stand firm. Stand firm therefore, having girded your loins with truth, and having put on the breastplate of righteousness, and having shod your feet with the preparation of the gospel of peace; in addition to all, taking up the shield of faith with which you will be able to extinguish all the flaming arrows of the evil one. And take the helmet of salvation, and the sword of the Spirit, which is the word of God. (Ephesians 6:10-17 NASB)

In this section of scripture I learned that I was in a battle. I was to remain strong in the Lord, in this battle, not in my flesh. I couldn't do it the normal, human way. People will make excuses for falling into temptation and succumbing to it's power. They will say that God made us human, with human impulses and urges and it's just natural to give in to them. What they fail to remember is God created mankind in a perfect environment, with perfect impulses and urges. When mankind rebelled against God, all that changed. Now our impulses are governed and influenced by our own sinful nature, or that belonging to others, and by satan (the devil mentioned in the above verses).

So if I couldn't trust my feelings, my impulses and even my own thoughts sometimes, what could I trust? I decided the only thing I could trust in my mind was God's Word. I took my memory verses and really put them to heart. David wrote,

> "In my heart I store up (or hide) your words, so I might not sin against you." (Psalms 119:11 NET)

I memorized 2 Corinthians 10:5 which reads,

> "We are destroying speculations and every lofty thing raised up against the knowledge of God, and we are taking every thought captive to the obedience of Christ," (2 Corinthians 10:5 NASB)

Each time a thought came to me that I knew was not pleasing to God or trustworthy, I would repeat those words, attempting to capture every thought and make it obedient to Christ.

To be obedient to Christ I had to know how and what Christ wants me to obey. Again, the Bible is the only thing we have that is proven trustworthy. As the psalmist I can attest:

> For this reason I love your commands more than gold, even purest gold. For this reason I carefully follow all your precepts. I hate all deceitful actions. (Psalms 119:127, 128 NET)

I studied the verses pertaining to marriage, love, unconditional love, endurance, etc. The one that cut me to the quick was one that I found in the book of Hebrews.

> "Marriage is to be held in honor among all, and the marriage bed is to be undefiled; for fornicators and adulterers God will judge." (Hebrews 13:4 NASB)

The Amplified Bible interprets it this way:

> "Let marriage be held in honor (esteemed worthy, precious, of great price, and especially dear) in all things. And thus let the marriage bed be undefiled (kept undishonored); for God will judge and punish the unchaste [all guilty of sexual vice] and adulterous. (Hebrews 13:4 AMP)

As I studied the words "fornicators" and "adulterers" I learned that the former had to do with sex before marriage and the latter had to do with sex after marriage, but not with one's own spouse. Many people, myself included at one time, believe that the Bible is old fashioned and not pertinent to today's culture. After all, we've had the "sexual revolution" and with the divorce rate so high, God can't expect us to just get married without living together first. We have to test the waters, so to speak.

That's the same old lie people have swallowed from the Father of Lies for millenniums. Cohabitation and divorce are not novel ideas. For example, Jesus, omnisciently proclaimed to the Samaritan woman He had met at a well that she had been married five times and the man she was living with at the time was not her husband. (John 4:17-18) Also, the disciples questioned Jesus when He he told them

> "...that whoever divorces his wife, except for immorality, and marries a n o t h e r c o m m i t s adultery." (Matthew 19:9 NET)

When asked why Moses put the terms for divorce into the Law, Jesus replied,...

> "Because of your hardness of heart Moses permitted you to divorce your wives; but from the beginning it has not been this way." (Matthew 19:8 NASB)

The beginning refers to Genesis and the creation of the first man and woman. Jesus said,

> "Have you not read that He who created them from the beginning made them male and female, and said, 'For this reason a man shall leave his father and mother and be joined to his wife, and the two shall become one flesh'? So they are no longer two, but one flesh. What therefore God has joined together, let no man separate." (Matthew 19:4-6 NASB)

Every generation believes it's got the new revelation on sex. Sexual immorality is found throughout scripture as early as Genesis, after the "fall of man" when we walked away from God's will and perfect ways into our own selfish desires and deeds.

The problem at this point in history is we've become so accustomed in our society to moral relativism that we don't know the truth, or if truth even exists. The definition that I found on the internet for moral relativism is "The philosophized notion that right and wrong are not absolute values, but are personalized according to the individual and his or her circumstances or cultural orientation." In a world where people think they are the sovereign rulers, that would be true, and in my opinion extremely confusing, due to so many differing thoughts, opinions, and personalities. In my world where I proclaim God as Sovereign Ruler I find comfort in knowing His Truth is trustworthy.

Now getting back to the scripture that says the marriage bed should remain undefiled. When I learned that verse and wanted to submit to the obedience of Christ I wondered how could I ever make it all right since I had already defiled the marriage bed by committing both fornication and adultery in my past. Even at that time I was struggling with committing adultery in my heart. Jesus had said,

> "You have heard that it was said, 'You shall not commit adultery '; but I say to you that everyone who looks at a woman with lust for her has already committed adultery with her in his heart." (Matthew 5:27, 28 NASB)

Even though this verse is for men, I can convert it to apply to women. Men lust after the flesh. Women lust after the romance. So if I'm thinking about any other man, real or imaginary, with romantic connotations I have already committed adultery with him.

I was convicted of my sin. In this sense the word convict means "to impress with a sense of guilt." What could I do? I remembered what Jesus said to the woman that was brought to him after she had been caught in adultery. He told her simply, "Go, and leave your sinful lifestyle." That's what repentance is. I've heard it described as while walking in one direction, stopping, making an about-face and going in the opposite direction. The opposite of adultery is faithfulness. I stopped following the lust of my heart and I devoted my thoughts to being a faithful wife to my husband.

The first chapter of 1 John is a wonderful little portion of the Bible that has a section that teaches us how to deal with sin.

> "If we say that we have fellowship with Him and yet walk in the darkness, we lie and do not practice the truth; but if we walk in the Light as He Himself is in the Light, we have fellowship with one another, and the blood of Jesus His Son cleanses us from all sin. If we say that we have no sin, we are deceiving ourselves and the truth is not in us. If we confess our sins, He is faithful and righteous to forgive us our sins and to cleanse us from all unrighteousness. (1 John 1:6-9 NASB)

This pretty much lays it down on the line. If I belong to Jesus, I should not want to sin. If I do sin, I have a recourse: confess it...quickly! And the beauty of the Lord is that He will forgive me, AND cleanse me. I've always loved this verse. I have such a small part to play in this transaction: confessing, which is agreeing with God that I have sinned. Though it's small, it's also the most difficult thing for human beings to do.

I help manage a pool with teen-age lifeguards. Often I will find a mistake or misstep that one has committed and my job is to let them know what they did wrong and explain the correct way to do it. Invariably the offending teen will make excuses as to why they did it wrongly or they will have detailed explanations as to the reason that in fact they did it correctly but it still came out incorrectly or that they didn't do it, someone else did. On the sweet occasion when one will realize the mistake and say, "Oh man, I'm sorry. I messed up there, didn't I? I'll do better next time." My heart soars with joy when that happens. If I love to hear that from these kids whom I love dearly, how much more would we bless God by confessing our sins! His love for us is much greater so we should always want to please Him.

So when we do confess and agree with the Lord the rest is up to Him. The verses promise that when we confess He is faithful, righteous and just to forgive us AND to cleanse us from all unrighteousness. I remind God often that He has promised to cleanse me from ALL unrighteousness. As those nasty "leeches" (see chapter 1) are revealed I know He's going to get rid of them. I can trust Him.

The Way He Teaches Me 10

1. Lies and temptation come at me from all directions, especially the media, whether digital or in book form.

2. When I am tempted I must use God's Word as a weapon against the lies and temptation.

3. If I fall into temptation, I have recourse through confession and trusting the Lord to forgive and cleanse me.

Chapter 11

BROKENNESS

"Christianity is mostly concerned with your death." (R.T. Kendall)

"Lord, whatever it takes...."

How many times have I prayed that over my life? I thought I really meant it when I prayed it. It seemed so good. It seemed so right and noble. I didn't think the answer to that prayer would bring so much pain into my life, but it did. I had been through trials before, but the latest series of these blindsided me and hit me so hard I wasn't sure I would recover.

There is a song on the radio with the line, "I guess we're all one phone call from our knees." Have you ever gotten that phone call? Life is hard. No question about that. I've always responded to those three words with "But God is good." The last few years of my life brought me to places where I started to question that last bit. I've heard it called a "crisis of faith". I've read about "brokenness", either in the lives of people in the Bible or fellow Christ-followers who have been through the refiners fire...and lived to tell about it.

As I read these written works I would absolutely, yet ignorantly, equate the suffering and anguish the authors described with my own difficult experiences. I'd be encouraged to endure and continue on. In my naiveté I thought I understood what suffering and brokenness meant. That was until I met my own personal crucible, the affliction that turned my world upside down. I have a feeling it's not the same for each person. What is a trial to me won't be difficult for another, and vice versa. That's the beauty of it. It's so customized that only a loving, good God could generate the perfect scenario with the ultimate result.

I've heard many preachers expound on the refiner's fire. They explained that when silver is mined from the earth it has so many impurities that one would never know there is silver hidden inside the nugget. The only way to get the silver out is to put it through the fire. The silver smith will put the unrefined silver into the melting pot, place it over hot coals and let it melt. As the process goes on the impurities float to the surface and the silver smith skims them off the top. He looks inside the pot and sees a dull reflection of himself. The fire needs to be turned up higher and more impurities rise to the surface to be skimmed off. He continues doing this until the time he looks inside the pot and sees a perfect reflection of himself.

Paul wrote

> "because those whom he foreknew he also predestined to be conformed to the image of his Son, that his Son would be the firstborn among many brothers and sisters." (Romans 8:29 NET)

As the refiner expects to see his own image in the refined silver, our Father longs for us to be "conformed to the image of His Son". As with silver, the surest method of refining is going through the fire. As painful as that sounds, I take comfort in some other facts about refining that I can apply to my life. For instance, the silver smith never leaves the pot alone on the fire. He knows that the moment he steps away something will go wrong. The silver is delicate and needs constant supervision. In that same respect, my Father will never leave me, nor forsake me.

> "God is our refuge and strength, an ever-present help in trouble." (Psalm 46:1 NIV)

Also, the smith will never turn the heat up more than is needed. He knows the precise temperature that will produce the best results. Similarly, God will never put me through trials or pain that are more than necessary. God is perfect. He is sovereign. He loves me. I can trust Him.

As I've stated before, Mark and I are not college graduates. We started out as bus drivers. All along through the years our needs were met, though we lived paycheck to paycheck. We have learned to live by faith. We had been abundantly blessed throughout the years and I was able to stay at home and home-school our children. By 2008 we had a wonderful life. The dealership where Mark worked was family owned, honest and very generous to their employees. We received so many perks, the best of which was a free all expense paid cruise to the Bahamas, which providentially occurred at the time of our twentieth anniversary. At home, we had moved into a lovely, old fashioned community where we knew our neighbors and enjoyed much interaction with them. Our home was surrounded by peace and beauty. At church, each of us experienced great fellowship as we served in various capacities. My husband was a trustee, enjoying great friendships with the pastors, elders and fellow trustees, as well as with many other members of the congregation. I knew 95% of the women in our church and felt connected to each. I was asked to be the director of the sound booth ministry. I became educated in all the technological aspects of church ministry, including becoming trained as a sound technician. I felt it was the ministry for which I was created. Both our son who was twenty-three years old, and our daughter, who was ten, served as musicians on the worship team. I felt blessed beyond measure.

The following year things started to change. The car manufacturer that employed my husband started showing signs of failure. Rumors had it that the factory would be closing. The company was going bankrupt. Mark's dealership had it's own problems. His pay was cut by forty percent.　On top of that, Mark's health had been compromised by a ninety-nine percent blocked artery. If you saw him you'd think he was the picture of perfect health. Working out at the gym has been his lifestyle as long as I've known him. Being fit and trim one would never suspect he'd have heart issues. A stent solved the problem but he would have to take very expensive medicine to keep things from getting worse.　The cost of living was rising due to the recession/economy and our pay was declining.

Our daughter was in eighth grade. We considered whether we should continue home-schooling or not and if I should find a job outside the home. At the same time my body decided to show signs of aging. Fatigue, pain, mental fog attacked me at varying levels. Some days were unbearable. Most days it was just annoying enough to keep me from enjoying life.　I had blood tests done which showed no cause.　Today I believe it was a combination of age, hormones and stress. Whatever it was it caused me great concern especially with the contemplation of possibly going out to work. I didn't feel capable of keeping any kind of long hours or of doing anything that needed my full mental faculties. I started feeling pretty useless. Mark's job situation and my physical limitations brought on stress and depression though I didn't realize it as such as it was very subtle at first.　I brought it to the Lord continually and I thought I had it under control.

We were being hit financially and physically. My consolation was our church.　Our ministries were thriving and we felt we were contributing to God's Kingdom and loving His people through them.　Through the teaching and fellowship at church we were growing and maturing in Christ with our fellow-believers. However at some point during this stressful period something started to change. Others noticed it before I did and there seemed to be a growing division.　I was not aware of the cause for some time, yet in my spirit I was suffering every time I went to church.　This caused more depression in my soul. My heart was heavy at home and heavy at church. I was confused and forlorn due to being financially, physically and now spiritually assailed. I felt as though my heart was being crushed in a huge vise.

The battle in my mind was relentless. Everything of which I thought my life consisted was being torn away. All I had left was my family: my husband and children. We started to regroup, seeking God as a family. As we did so the situation at church worsened resulting in the resignation from our ministries. Eventually we left our beloved church family.

The months that followed were treacherous. Grieving the great loss in my life caused severe depression that led to suicidal thoughts. My husband was dealing with his struggling job situation and was unable to help me. I sought counseling. As a family we visited different churches. I felt some relief from the pain but it was never completely healed. Something always seemed to trigger a setback. At one of my lowest points I was attacked emotionally one more time. This time the attack was against my family life, the only thing I had left. It almost undid me.

There was a man at church who had been a great comfort and support to Mark and me as we were going through the financial setbacks and discouragement. He had been through his own "crucible", lost everything and was coming back, growing in faith and repentance. He told us once that we sing some dangerous songs. You know the type, the ones that have us singing: "Take All of Me", "Empty me of me", "I Surrender All", "Whatever it takes, I'll trust You completely, I'm here in Your hands if You need to break me." (Nothing Back, by Chelsea Boyd) He said he used to sing those songs and God actually did what he sang. He lost everything that he thought was important. He learned anew what was really important. This friend gave us scripture, encouraging us to memorize the Word of God for our comfort and endurance through the trials. At some point before we left the church I had heard he had moved down to his winter residence due to the nature of his employment.

A few months after we left the church, out of the blue, he contacted me proclaiming he was in love with me. I was flabbergasted and confused, and yes, a little flattered. I told him flat out this was just satan's lies and he had to forget about it and move on. Mark spoke with him and realizing he was inebriated told him not to contact me any longer. We blocked his number from my phone and I thought that was the end of it.

In my fragile state that incident caused even more consternation. This man had been one of our main sources of encouragement because I was led to believe he had "lost everything" and had come back to faith in full force. Now that all seemed to be a lie. The doubts crept in like slithering rats. My thoughts went places they've never gone before. If the truth of God's word hadn't been enough for him, if it didn't work for him, why should I believe it would work for me? Maybe everything I believed in was a sham. I tried desperately to keep my thoughts conformed to God's Word but the depression was too dark. I lost sense of all that was true and good.

A few weeks later I had a major setback--thoughts of hopelessness and despair pervading my mind. Mark, dealing with his own frustration and worry was distant, unable to see the pain which enveloped me. No one seemed to care and I spiraled downward in my despondency. I thought of this man and wondered if he had come to his senses. I had to find out. If he had, maybe there was hope. I contacted him. I knew it was wrong but I didn't care because my whole life seemed wrong at this point.

The conversation that proceeded assailed me with every temptation that could possibly take me out. In the last chapter I spoke of the temptations of my mind, thoughts of what I wanted in romance and security. This man promised it all to me, twisting scripture to back up his proposals, stating that divorce was allowed and God wants you to get "the desires of your heart". My mind battled with thoughts of running away and leaving my shattered life just to ease the pain.

One thought kept interrupting the chaos. "Make your heart completely Mine" (from 2 Chronicles 16:9). Jesus was calling me. HE was romancing me offering me hope and a future. I didn't realize it at the time but looking back Jesus was trying to teach me that I don't need nor should I desire any man to meet my needs: not a friend, nor a pastor, nor a co-worker, nor even a husband! However, in the middle of this conversation I hadn't come to that realization yet. One thing did occur to me: I had made a tremendous mistake in making this phone call. I gave this man cause for hope, that I might take him up on his proposition and when I started to falter, coming to my senses, in desperation he threatened to come after me, "full court press". Fear captivated my heart: fear of him bringing his threats to life, fear of what Mark would do when he found out I had contacted this man again, and even, fear of what this man, whom I still considered a friend, would do to himself. I finally ended the conversation with these words, "I am going to hang up now and I'm either going to tell Mark what I did or I'm going to kill myself." I was quite serious, however, thankfully, I decided on the former. Jesus said,

> "If you grasp and cling to life on your terms, you'll lose it, but if you let that life go, you'll get life on God's terms."
> Luke 17:31-33 *The Message*)

I knew that if I tried to strive for what I thought would make me happy I'd miss out on what God knows will bring me great joy. No pain, no gain, at least in this instance.

I gathered the nerve and told Mark what I had done. Mark was angry, as would be expected. He called the man and warned him to stay away. We talked, calmed down and my husband, showed me what true love does. He forgave me, then made suggestions, demands and actually helped me get through my despair. I was amazed how this was actually bringing us closer together. Mark got the wake up call that his wife needed help and if he didn't provide it someone else was willing to. He had always seen me as the strong Christian woman. As my weaknesses became more apparent to both of us I was reminded of the Bible verse, where Paul stated,

> "But He said to me, 'My grace is enough for you, for my power is made perfect in weakness.' So then, I will boast most gladly about my weaknesses, so that the power of Christ may reside in me." (2 Corinthians 12:9 NET)

It was somewhere around this time that our Father revealed to me that everything I had been going through, the great loss I had endured at this time that was causing me heart - wrenching grief, was all in answer to a prayer I had prayed about 20 years earlier. I had prayed, "Lord, do whatever it takes to make Mark the man of God you want him to be."

And I recalled the words He responded with were, "Are you ready for what it takes?"

I pondered that question, thinking the worst, and yet, sensibly answered, "Lord, make me ready."

As I recollected this conversation with the Lord I was filled with awe at the power of prayer in my life, once again contemplating the perfect timing of God's answer. He truly has made me "ready", ready as I ever could be to have the rug pulled out from under me...absolutely. Insightfully I knew that if it had happened any earlier it would have been very detrimental.

Paul said:

> "Now those who belong to Christ have crucified the flesh with its passions and desires." (Galatians 5:24 NET)

Missionary and martyr Jim Elliot said:

"He is no fool who gives what he cannot keep to gain that which he cannot lose."

Jesus warned us that following Him could be costly. It could cost us our jobs, our family and friends and even our lives. It cost me my "comfort zone". I lost almost everything that was important and comfortable to me. I lost what I thought I knew to be "true". I am very grateful that I didn't lose my family or my home, which I know some folks have, but what I did lose meant more to me than I even realized. The astonishing thing is that the things I lost, like my church work, ministries and fellowship, weren't sinful things. They were good things that I know the Lord had given me, for which He had anointed and appointed me. It was all a wonderful season of my life. Then, just as the Lord gave, He took it away. As Job said,

> "Naked I came from my mother's womb, and naked I will return there. The Lord gives, and the Lord takes away. May the name of the Lord be blessed!" (Job 1:21 NET)

For months after I had suffered this great loss, experiencing terrific bouts of depression, I realized I was going through the grief process just as one would if they lost a loved one. I encountered some of the stages of grief people often describe such as shock or denial, anger, bargaining and depression. I had suffered from depression earlier in my life but never to this extent and potency. The pain was mental, physical and emotional. It wasn't so bad that I couldn't get out of bed, which is the case for some people. I could barely function but I did function. My "gumption" was gone. I had no interest in life other than trying to meet my family's needs as best as I could under the circumstances.

I have to admit that before I went through this I ignorantly and slightly arrogantly advised folks to deal with depression through Bible study, prayer and deliverance through the laying on of hands by an elder or pastor. I don't disagree with that advice; however, I now know there is so much more. God created us in His image and like Him we have three parts that make the whole. We have a body which is physical, a soul which consists of the mind, will and emotions, and a spirit which is the part which connects with God, the Holy Spirit. Depression invades each of those areas and each invasion needs to be dealt with.

Depression is a mental, or emotional, illness. It attacks our soul, the seat of emotion, and our thoughts. Counseling is a good antidote. Professional counselors are able to find the root causes and help counter the onslaught of negative thinking. I sought a Christian counselor, one who is known for successful outcomes. Prayer before seeking professional help has resulted in finding some perfect matches for our situations.

Depression is also a physical phenomenon. There may be a chemical imbalance or hormonal situation causing feelings of discouragement or anxiety. Stress releases hormones and attacks adrenal glands that cause all sorts of imbalances and physical problems. There is more to this than I'll ever know. This area should be treated by a doctor or professional. Perhaps a nutritionist would help. Again, prayer for direction is imperative. For me progesterone cream was the answer.

Spiritually, depression is an attack from the devil and his cohorts, the enemies of our Lord Jesus Christ. Those crippling thoughts of discouragement and despair come from him. In the Bible when Saul, the first King of Israel, walked away from God and His ways, a tormenting spirit bothered him constantly. The only thing that soothed his spirit was the music from a harp played by a young shepherd named David, who unbeknownst to either of them would be Saul's successor. Spiritual attacks require spiritual warfare. Ephesians chapter six gives us a detailed list of our armor and weapons we can use for this battle. Reading this list has helped me overcome many onslaughts of the devil in my life.

"Clothe yourselves with the full armor of God so that you may be able to stand against the schemes of the devil. For our struggle is not against flesh and blood, but against the rulers, against the powers, against the world rulers of this darkness, against the spiritual forces of evil in the heavens. For this reason, take up the full armor of God so that you may be able to stand your ground on the evil day, and having done everything, to stand. Stand firm therefore, by fastening the belt of truth around your waist, by putting on the breastplate of righteousness, by fitting your feet with the preparation that comes from the good news of peace, and in all of this, by taking up the shield of faith with which you can extinguish all the flaming arrows of

> the evil one. And take the helmet of
> salvation and the sword of the Spirit,
> which is the word of God. With every
> prayer and petition, pray at all times
> in the Spirit, and to this end be alert,
> with all perseverance and requests
> for all the saints." (Ephesians 6:11-18
> NET)

I will admit there were times that I couldn't even pick up my Bible much less read one word of it. The hopelessness and confusion captivated my thoughts. I couldn't even pray. However, there was one statement that found it's way to my lips and I would say it over and over. "Jesus, I trust you." At my darkest moments I summoned all my strength, which wasn't much, just to say those four words. Even though I didn't understand what I was going through and even at that moment I didn't realize it was spiritual attack I just knew I could trust Jesus. Or as one of my friends fondly declares, "He is safe to trust." My thoughts cleared enough that I could reason that this was only temporary. Even if nothing changed, and it even got worse, eventually when I did die, I would be with Jesus in perfect peace, and no more pain. I knew one thing without a doubt, that as Paul stated,

> "This saying is trustworthy and
> deserves full acceptance: 'Christ
> Jesus came into the world to save
> sinners' – and I am the worst of them!
> " (1 Timothy 1:15 NET)

This was the truth that got me through the toughest of times that even if I were the worst sinner, Christ died for me and saved me from eternal destruction. Hopelessness is one of the worst feelings I've ever experienced. Because I have put my faith in Jesus, the Word of God, I had hope even when I thought I was hopeless.

"... we who have taken refuge would have strong encouragement to take hold of the hope set before us. This hope we have as an anchor of the soul, a hope both sure and steadfast...", (Hebrews 6:18b, 19a NASB)

"...because of the hope laid up for you in heaven," (Colossians 1:5 NASB)

"Let us hold fast the confession of our hope without wavering, for He who promised is faithful;" (Hebrews 10:23 NASB)

I've titled this chapter Brokenness. As I think of that word I think of a wild horse and how it is "broken" in order to become a useful member on a ranch. I can see now how my Father used this time of brokenness to help me become a more useful member in His family. I understand pain and suffering a little better. I am much more humble in the area of thinking I have my life all figured out. I also have learned more about compassion, trust, and the importance of resting in the Lord.

In her book Brokenness Nancy Leigh DeMoss says, "True brokenness is a lifestyle--a moment-by-moment lifestyle of agreeing with God about the true condition of my heart and life--not as everyone else thinks it is but as He knows it to be.

Brokenness is the shattering of my self-will--the absolute surrender of my will to the will of God. It is saying 'Yes, Lord!'--no resistance, no chafing, no stubbornness--simply submitting myself to His direction and will in my life."

Paul wrote,

> "For I am sure of this very thing, that the one who began a good work in you will perfect it until the day of Christ Jesus." (Philippians 1:6 NET)

At the end of this chapter I have added the lyrics to a song by Jars of Clay that has resonated with my spirit for years. I had prayed it as I sang along. I believe God answered me. I'm glad He did.

I trust His work, which includes brokenness, to bring me to where He wants me to be. He is sovereign and He is good!

The Way He Teaches Me 11

1. The trials in my life can be used to refine me as a smith's fire refines the precious metal hidden inside the dirt.

2. In order to save my life, I have to lose it.

3. No matter what happens in this life, I can trust Jesus will take perfect care of me, and in the end I will be with Him in perfect peace.

4. Depression hits all three areas of our being, physical, emotional and spiritual, and each must be treated.

"Worlds Apart"
written by Stephen Daniel Mason, Charlie Lowell, Dan Haseltine, Matt Odmark
Lyrics © Universal Music Publishing Group

I am the only one to blame for this
Somehow it all ends up the same
Soaring on the wings
of selfish pride
I flew too high
and like Icarus I collide
With a world I try so hard
to leave behind
To rid myself of all but love
to give and die
To turn away and not become
Another nail to pierce the skin
of one who loves
more deeply than the oceans,
more abundant than the tears
Of a world embracing
every heartache
Can I be the one to sacrifice
Or grip the spear and watch
the blood and water flow

To love you - take my world apart
To need you - I am on my knees
To love you - take my world apart
To need you -broken on my knees

All said and done I stand alone
Amongst remains of a life
I should not own
It takes all I am to believe
In the mercy that covers me

Did you really have to die for me?
All I am for all you are
Because what I need and what
I believe are worlds apart

look beyond the empty cross
forgetting what my life has cost
and wipe away
the crimson stains
and dull the nails that still remain
More and more I need you now,
I owe you more
each passing hour
the battle between
grace and pride
I gave up not so long ago
So steal my heart
and take the pain
and wash the feet
and cleanse my pride
take the selfish, take the weak,
and all the things I cannot hide
take the beauty, take my tears
the sin-soaked heart
and make it yours
take my world all apart
take it now, take it now
and serve the ones
that I despise
speak the words I can't deny
watch the world I used to love
fall to dust and thrown away
I look beyond the empty cross
forgetting what my life has cost
so wipe away the crimson stains
and dull the nails that still remain
so steal my heart
and take the pain
take the selfish, take the weak
and all the things I cannot hide
take the beauty, take my tears
take my world apart,
I pray, I pray, I pray
take my world apart

Chapter 12

VICTORY

"for everyone born of God overcomes the world. This is
the victory that has overcome the world, even our faith."

(1 John 5:4)

I had a fight with my husband during the time
that I was writing the last chapter. Well, it was not really a
fight; more like a strong disagreement and a familiar
disagreement, at that. I thought to myself, "That's it. I'm not
taking this anymore. I'm done. Things are going to be
different from now on." The problem is, those thoughts were
familiar, too. I sat there thinking about this book. I knew the
next chapter was going to be entitled Victory because I had
thought through the titles before writing the chapters. The
titles came to me easily and I had glimpses or parts of the
chapters in mind for all of them except the last one. I just
knew it was supposed to have the title "Victory" but I had no
idea what it would contain. As I sat there feeling defeated
after my argument with Mark, I thought, "Well that settles it. I
can't even finish writing this book. I don't feel victorious at
all."

I have often told people, especially those going through
trials, that Christ has given them everything they need to be
victorious. Some people would say that God only gives us
what we can handle. I disagree with that. As I've been
learning over the years, my own strength is useless. I can't
handle anything! However, through Christ, leaning on Him,
waiting on Him and trusting Him to work everything together
for my good, I can do all things. (according to Philippians
4:13) It is really Christ doing it through me.

As I sat there debating over chucking this book into the trash bin I had an epiphany. I remembered how my thoughts over the past two years have run amuck along with my emotions. One minute everything was hunky dory and then a short time later I thought my life was worthless. One minute I was enamored with my husband, the next I wanted to buy him a one way ticket to anywhere. I was happy then I was sad. All sorts of feelings and emotions wreaked havoc with me throughout the previous months. I came to the conclusion, that I could not trust what I was thinking or feeling. I had to decide what was the truth and concentrate on that when I got into that wrong place. Before Jesus was taken away to be crucified he prayed for his disciples and all who would believe because of their testimony about Jesus. That includes us in the 21st century. He asked His Father to "Sanctify them in the truth; Your word is truth." (John 17:17 NASB) Sanctify means to set apart; consecrate; separate unto God; make holy. When I am having these episodes of depression or confusion I need to consecrate or sanctify my thoughts in the truth. God's Word is truth.

I am a firm believer in memorizing scripture. David wrote: "Your word I have treasured in my heart, that I may not sin against You." (Psalms 119:11 NASB) When my children were young they participated in activities at church that were based on memorizing scripture. Recently I realized we had become lax in that area. It's much easier to memorize when we are younger. I recently purchased some books to help us get back on that track. I am very thankful I had learned to memorize scripture when I was a new believer. During these last few years of trials that have been worse than any I've experienced previously those scriptures came to mind. Psalm 23 and the Lord's Prayer have been my comfort and solace, helping me get to sleep many nights. Romans 6 has been a long time persuader in my life, keeping me on the right track when faced with temptation. "What shall we say then? Shall we continue in sin that grace may abound? God forbid! How shall we who are dead to sin live any longer therein." I just typed that from memory, having memorized it thirty years ago. It comes back to mind like a favorite nursery rhyme.

We have everything we need to be victorious. We have the Word of God. We also have the Holy Spirit. Here is what Jesus said about the Holy Spirit:

> "If you love me, you will obey my commandments. Then I will ask the Father, and he will give you another Advocate to be with you forever – the Spirit of truth, whom the world cannot accept, because it does not see him or know him. But you know him, because he resides with you and will be in you. 'I will not abandon you as orphans, I will come to you.'" (John 14:15-18 NET)

If I love Jesus I will obey his commandments. I need to know what those commandments are in order to obey them. Those commandments are found in the Bible. If I claim to love Jesus but never read the Bible, I can't obey Him therefore I don't love Him. "If you love me, you will obey my commandments. Then..." The passage indicates that first comes the love and obedience, then comes the gift of the "Advocate", who is the Holy Spirit. Different words used in other versions are Helper, Counselor and Comforter, all of which have problems in English to describe this unique and incredibly important Person of the Trinity. The Holy Spirit is God; the part of God that meets my spirit, brought it to life at the moment I believed, and continues to live in me throughout this life on earth. The Spirit teaches me, guides me, brings me under conviction of sin, reminds me of God's Word and truth and communicates God's love to me.

Because I have the Holy Spirit that Jesus promised, I have what I need to be victorious. However, Paul warns us:

> "Do not quench (suppress or subdue) the [Holy] Spirit;" (1 Thessalonians 5:19 AMP)

I can do that...quench the Holy Spirit in my life. I used to do it quite often. When I first became a believer I couldn't believe that God's ways would bring me happiness. I wanted to feel good, have fun, and that didn't always line up with God's Word. So when the Holy Spirit would nudge me that I was about to do something I shouldn't, I quenched Him. The outcome was never good. Like the Prodigal Son I'd have to come crawling back, ask forgiveness and try not to quench Him in the future. At this point in my life I'm very careful to listen, seek and wait for the guidance of the Holy Spirit. I've learned the hard way that His way is best.

As I was contemplating the latest argument with my husband, with the knowledge that I could not trust my emotions and thoughts all the time, I decided to focus on the truth. The truth about my marriage and the truth about God's plan. The first thing that came to mind is based on Romans 3:23, all people are sinners. Mark is a sinner, acting selfishly at times, but he is also married to a selfish sinner, me. He and I have always been at odds because of our personality differences. When our personalities collide we hurt each other. For the extent of our marriage I have tried desperately to make our marriage free from conflicts. I thought that was the sign of the perfect marriage. During my epiphany I changed my thinking. It's not the conflicts that are the problem. It's what I let those conflicts do to my heart, my mindset. Usually the process after a conflict would be: "See, I just can't live with him. We'll never be compatible." However, a quote I had recently read changed my thought patterns: Peace is not absence of conflict, it is the ability to handle conflict by peaceful means. (Google just told me that it was Ronald Reagan who said it.)

I am resigned to the fact that Mark and I will always have conflict. I have to decide what I will do with that knowledge. If I left Mark, and found someone else, knowing my personality, I will have conflict with them as well. However, the conflict with Mark after almost thirty years is familiar and manageable. I would really hate to have to start over and learn new strategies and behavior patterns. I'm just too old for that. As I was thinking these things, the hurt dissipated more quickly than usual and I forgave Mark. I did so in my heart, since he didn't even know I was so upset with him. I am also learning that not spouting off my thoughts right away can make a huge difference. Knowing when to speak and when to keep silent--what a difficult concept! That's where the Holy Spirit is a wonderful Helper.

Since that argument, which happened several weeks ago, it's been like our marriage has been re-born. There's a renewed love in my heart that is stronger than anything I have known before. Amazing love! Isn't that interesting? I change my mind and heart and my marriage gets a new lease on life. God's ways are so much better than mine.

I have two more very personal stories to share that have been great examples in my life of the sovereign love God has for me. Both involve others, my dad and my son, and I have obtained their permission to add them to my story. I am sharing these in hopes that others who have gone through similar situations may be confident of the truth in God's Word that we are more than conquerors through Him who loved us. (Romans 8:37) The Lord uses all things to work together for good for us who love Him.

I've shared that growing up with my adoptive father was painful. He wasn't the worst father when I was younger, not in the least, but he didn't have the tools to be an effective and loving father. He was angry and often unreasonable. I was the first born and therefore received the disadvantages of immature parenting. As a parent now, I see how the first born is the one with whom we make the most mistakes. Add to this the fact that my father had his own sin nature, his own childhood issues, and God was not in his life. None of this excuses what he did, I just want to set the background.

When I was sixteen years old my adoptive father, the only dad I knew, molested me by touching me inappropriately. I was able to escape quickly but the thought in my mind was that my dad was trying to have sexual relations with me. It was frightening, confusing and disheartening to say the least. I didn't tell anyone. The rest of my time at home was miserable and I left the day after graduation. I stayed with my friend's family in their small apartment until I left to go to nursing school.

After I was married to Mark I found my relationship with my father had been very dysfunctional over the years. I was always trying to convince him to love me, only ending up hurt and rejected. As I grew in Christian truth I learned to give him up to the Lord and pray for his salvation. One time when I knew my father and I were going to be together with other family members I felt the urge to pray for strength and wisdom. I'm thankful I chose to listen to that still small voice because as it turned out a situation occurred that angered my father greatly. We ended up in a very heated argument that led to me giving my father the same ultimatum I gave Mark years earlier. I told him I loved him and asked him if he wanted to be my father. He replied that he should have divorced me when he divorced my mother. My response was calm and collected, only by God's grace. I told him that was fine, that when he wanted to be my father again he could let me know. I couldn't force him to love me. I left and for years I didn't communicate with him. Even at family gatherings I avoided contact. It wasn't an angry action. It was just a matter of fact action, as though I didn't know him.

Fast forward to 1995 and we were living in Colorado. At a counseling session with a Christian counselor I learned to forgive all the people in my life that had hurt, offended or abused me. The counselor told me that forgiveness isn't a feeling; it's an act of my will. I choose to forgive just as God has forgiven me. I gave my dad over to God completely and forgave him, meaning I didn't hold his sin against him in my heart. I chose to let God deal with him because He could do it perfectly, better than I ever could. God doesn't let anyone off the hook. Sin has to be dealt with, one way or another. When I put my faith in Christ Jesus, my sin was dealt with on the cross. If I hadn't I would bear the burden of my sin forever. Forgiveness means I have no bitter feelings against that person again. It does not mean I have to let the person continue to abuse me. It means I take a stand, continue to love, perhaps from a distance and let God be the judge providing the consequences to that person. That is exactly what happened with my dad.

After we moved back to New Jersey we had a family gathering where I saw my father again. He walked up to me and started a conversation. He had never done that before. In the past, I had to pursue him, usually feeling dejected afterwards. Now it seemed God was beginning to heal our relationship. In the years that followed our relationship was amiable and pleasant.

One day in 2005, I called my dad to invite him to look at a house Mark and I were interested in purchasing. He seemed a little confused, told me he'd think about it and call me back later. I hung up, puzzled, but not discouraged. Our relationship had become secure enough that I didn't take it as rejection. Earlier in my life I would have. A little while later the phone rang. It was my dad and he asked me why I had called. I told him it was because I thought he would like this house we were looking at. He said, "No, really. Why did you call?" Now I was nonplussed! I figured he thought I needed money or something and that I was being devious in some manner. I tried convincing him of the truth. Finally he explained.

He told me he had been sleeping when I called the first time. I interrupted a dream he was having. In the dream he said his granddaughter was accusing him, saying, "I know what you did." Then he proceeded to apologize for abusing me when I was sixteen. As I realized what he was saying I started crying. I told him how I had forgiven him years earlier because I learned of God's love and forgiveness through Jesus Christ.

A few days after this conversation, through a series of circumstances, my father was admitted to the hospital. When my pastor visited him and explained the Good News of salvation through Jesus' death on the cross and resurrection into new life, my dad prayed with him and trusted Christ as his savior. Our relationship grew even sweeter after that and over the years I've learned, once again, that God's grace is truly amazing.

The second story took place when our son, Chris, was twenty years old. Because he and I had enjoyed attending the Macy's Thanksgiving Day parade years earlier I wanted to take Amy to the event that year. I asked Chris to go with us as I didn't feel comfortable taking a seven year old into the city by myself when there would be such great numbers of people. Mark didn't enjoy the city as we did so Chris was my choice of companion.

Chris is a musician and at the time he was frequenting clubs and bars to play at open mic sessions or run the sound for different venues. He was underage but he assured me he wasn't drinking alcohol and it was all fine. Our schedules were conflicting as he would often arrive home in the early hours of the morning and sleep until after noon. I wasn't happy with this lifestyle but I tried to be understanding. However, in my spirit I was agitated. I didn't know why but I knew in my heart something was wrong. I prayed for him diligently. My greatest concern was that we had a young daughter who I was trying to raise in the "glory and admonition of the Lord". It got so disconcerting that I wanted him to leave. I had nothing tangible to warrant this. I just "knew". I shared my concerns with our pastor one day and his advice to me seemed absurd at the time as he said, "You are praying. Don't worry. God's discipline is gentle, yet effective." I had already imagined "God's discipline", and it was pretty gruesome. I imagined Chris losing a limb or being paralyzed or some terrible thing God would use to get his attention. My image of God's discipline was pretty harsh. I don't know why I thought so since He had always been so gentle and merciful with me. Maybe I arrogantly felt Chris was a tougher nut to crack than I was. I had heard too many stories where people didn't listen to the Father's calling until some tragedy occurred. I'm so thankful God's ways are much better than ours.

On this Thanksgiving Eve, Chris had planned to go to a bar with his friends and agreed to be home early so we could catch the 5 a.m. bus to New York City. I awoke a little after 1:30 a.m. and as I looked at the clock I thought, "I wonder if Chris is home." Then I decided I didn't want to know because if he wasn't I'd just be frustrated and wouldn't get enough sleep. It wasn't more than five minutes later that the phone rang. Chris was on the other end, screaming. He was saying something about flipping his car. My heart pounded through my chest. As I repeated his words Mark jumped out of bed, asking where Chris was. As I obtained Chris' location and kept talking with Chris, Mark got dressed and headed out the door to meet him. The next two hours blurred together as I waited and prayed. When they finally walked through the door Chris was crying and proclaiming his life was over. The first words out of my mouth were, "No Honey, the Lord disciplines those He loves!" emphasizing the word "loves". His reply was, "I know. I have been thinking that all night."

As the story unfolded I sat in awe at the grace that had been poured out on us once again. Chris told us he was having a good time with his friends and as it was Thanksgiving Eve people were buying him beers. He assured us he had only a few over a long period of time and he felt completely sober enough to drive home. That was his story and he was sticking to it. As he drove home, however, he made the unwise decision to type a text message to a friend. When he did so, eyes off the road, his car veered to the right, hit a low rock wall and flipped over onto the driver's side leaving Chris stunned, sitting in a pile of glass with the airbag in his face. As he relayed to me what happened, my heart raced and my mind spun with anxious thoughts of how close my son had come to a severe tragedy.

In the morning Chris awoke, repentant and forlorn. I reminded him that the circumstances could have been much worse. Thankfully, no one was hurt, and no one else's property was damaged, not even the rock wall. Chris didn't have a scratch on him. I expected there to be bruises or scratches from the seat belt and airbag, as I've heard was the case by so many others who were in accidents. His car was totaled--his car, which he had just purchased recently and for which he had a personal loan. Three tickets were issued: one for driving under the influence, one for reckless driving, and one for texting while driving. All of the consequences from this accident were going to be solely financial and emotional. He would have to pay for a car he no longer possessed, and also, somehow obtain another car. Also, he'd lose his license for six months and pay thousands of dollars in fines. My pastor's words echoed in my ears, "God's discipline is gentle, yet effective."

As we sat in our living room that Thanksgiving morning, contemplating all that had transpired, I noticed something on the three tickets. The numbers 143 have carried a special significance to our family since Amy was young and watched Mr. Rogers' Neighborhood. He used those numbers in an episode explaining that it stood for "I love you" because there is one letter in I, four letters in love and three in you. We used it frequently and it has become a symbol of God's love to me over the years as I will see it in the most unique places and at perfect times. This was one of them. The numbers were on each of the three tickets--in the space for the officer's badge number. The cop's badge number was 143! When I saw this I declared to Chris, "Look! God is saying He loves you, three times! just like He did to Peter, (the apostle)."

I continued to encourage him as I reminded him of God's plan for his life. I said, "I believe God has a great plan for you. Satan wants to stop that plan and you almost let him tonight, by your foolishness. However, I believe that you are alive today because your dad prays for your protection every morning before he leaves for work." Chris was encouraged, and later that day he created a webpage with photos from the accident, which started with the words, "Don't drink and drive" and ended with a photo of himself and his dad with the caption, "I'm alive today because this guy prays for my protection every day." Chris took the wake up call and got his life back on track. God had answered my prayers and today I thank Him profusely for His gentle yet effective discipline.

When I began this book over a year ago I was still in the middle of one of the worst seasons of my life. My faith was tested every day. I was full of fear, doubting that all things really would work together for my good. Today as I come to the last pages of my writing I attest to God's faithfulness and goodness in my life. His blessings have been poured out on my family and me--physically, emotionally and spiritually. My heart is filled with joy unfathomable. Some days I cannot contain it and literally dance around with praise music blaring giving God the adoration of which He is so worthy!

Jesus said,

> "I have told you these things so that in Me you may have peace. In the world you have trouble and suffering, but take courage – I have conquered the world." (John 16:33 NET)

Paul wrote:

> No, in all these things we have complete victory through him who loved us! (Romans 8:37 NET)

> But thanks be to God, who gives us the victory through our Lord Jesus Christ! (1 Corinthians 15:57 NET)

I hope and pray that the readers of this book will see that the reason I share the stories of my weaknesses, failures and sins is so that they can get a glimpse of the way the Lord has provided His power and grace to work in my life, in spite of myself. I will always be amazed at the way He loves me.

"Now to Him who is able to do exceedingly abundantly above all that we ask or think, according to the power that works in us, to Him be glory in the church by Christ Jesus to all generations, forever and ever. Amen" Ephesian 3:20-21 (NKJV)

The Way He Teaches Me 12

1. In Christ, I have everything I need to be victorious.

2. God has given me His Word and His Holy Spirit to keep me on the right track.

3. God's discipline is gentle yet effective.

Mark's Song

by Dawna Renne (circa 1990)

originally wood-burned on a piece of oak

We were wild and crazy
Back when we first met.
You were oh so charming.
I never will forget
How you had me melting
In your skillful hand
I beheld you as my prince
Ah-Love was so grand

Then we came to reality
With the baby and the bills
Pressures got the best of us
Our love had lost it's thrills
But God in His merciful love
Carried us through that pain
We have learned to sift out the bad
And let the good remain

Though we had some hard times
That seemed our love would end
We stuck it out and I'm glad we did
For in you I've found my best friend
You may not be the man I wanted,
The one planned out in my head
You're far more better in every way
You're the man I needed instead

You're the guy who fixes my car
Shovels the snow and rakes the yard
You're the one who gives me hugs
When the day's been long and hard
You're the guy who brings home the milk
And tucks our son in at night
You're the one who humbles me
When I think I'm always right

And now I can honestly say
I'll love you my whole life long
I've learned that love means commitment
And God has made my commitment strong

THE WAY HE LOVES ME

Appendix A

Resources

✷ Marriage Without Regrets by Joyce Meyer

✷ Strike the Original Match by Chuck Swindol

✷ Improving Your Serve by Chuck Swindol

✷ Created to be a Help Meet by Debbie Pearl

✷ Love Must Be Tough by Dr. James Dobson

✷ Emotions: Can you Trust Them by Dr. James Dobson

✷ Love for a Lifetime by Dr. James Dobson

✷ Love and Respect by Dr. Emerson Eggerichs

✷ I Promise by Dr. Gary Smalley

✷ The Five Love Languages by Gary Chapman

✷ Lies Women Believe: And the Truth that Sets them Free by Nancy Leigh DeMoss

✷ The Bait of Satan by John Bevere

THE WAY HE LOVES ME

Made in the USA
Charleston, SC
22 October 2014